ENDLESS PATH

Celtic Myth

This is a **FLAME TREE** book
First published in 2007

Publisher and Creative Director: Nick Wells
Art Director: Mike Spender
Designer: Lucy Robins
Picture Research: Gemma Walters
Senior Editor: Cat Emslie
Production: Chris Herbert and Claire Walker
Proofreader: Siobhan O'Connor
Indexer: Helen Snaith

Special thanks to: Phillip A. Bernhardt-House, Chelsea Edwards and Toria Lyle

FLAME TREE PUBLISHING
Crabtree Hall, Crabtree Lane
Fulham, London SW6 6TY
United Kingdom
www.flametreepublishing.com

08 10 11 09 07
1 3 5 7 9 10 8 6 4 2

Flame Tree is part of The Foundry Creative Media Company Limited
Copyright © The Foundry 2007

A copy of the CIP data for this book is available from the British Library.

ISBN: 978-1-84451-743-5

Every effort has been made to contact copyright holders. In the event of an oversight
the publishers would be glad to rectify any omissions in future editions of this book.

Printed in China

ENDLESS PATH

Celtic Myth

Author: Kevin Eyres

Consultant: Rev. Dr Phillip A. Bernhardt-House

**FLAME TREE
PUBLISHING**

Contents

A Sprawling Collection: Gods, Goddesses, Heroes and Heroines 94

Battles, Voyages and Romance: The Myths 204

Introduction

I was a listener in the woods,
I was a gazer at the stars,
I was silent in the wilderness,
I was talkative among many...
Cormac mac Airt, Legendary high king of Tara

To appreciate the myths and legends of the Celts it is useful to put them into their historical context. The Celts seem to have emerged as a definable group early in the second millennium BC, making them possibly the first historically recorded European people north of the Alps. They seem to have made their home and begun to develop a distinct and recognizable culture in what we now know as Switzerland and Southern Germany.

The Celts were the one of the first people to perfect the process of iron smelting, and their ability to produce iron implements, especially axes and swords, gave them an immediate and tangible advantage over their neighbours. Celtic warriors were not slow to exploit their superiority and began expanding both north into Germany, and south over the Alps. At the same time as their iron axes and swords were carving out great swathes of Europe, their iron ploughshares were making Celtic farmers some of the most productive in Europe.

At the height of their power Celts held sway across Europe and as far east as Asia Minor. Indeed in c. 309 BC a group of Gauls (the Celts of the western European continent) attacked Rome, occupying it for six months until the Romans agreed to pay a significant ransom for the Gauls to depart. With the rise of the Roman Empire to the south and the Germanic and Slav tribes to the north, Celtic expansion ended in the first century BC. From then on the Celts migrated west to settle in what we commonly think of as the Celtic regions of Brittany, Ireland, Scotland, Wales and the Isle of Man.

Throughout this period the Celts were not one homogeneous group but rather a loose confederation of tribes sharing a common culture and languages (and regional dialects). What they did have in common was a love of feasting, storytelling and fighting. They had a well-developed belief in reincarnation and immortality and this made them fearless in battle. They also placed great value in craftsmanship and had a remarkable ability to produce exquisite jewellery, armour and weaponry.

Celtic culture survives to the present day in two distinct forms, which relate to a division of the Celtic language into two distinct branches. One, referred to as Goidelic, which first appeared in Ogham inscriptions around the second century AD, is spoken by Irish, Scottish and Manx Celts, whereas the Welsh, Cornish and Breton Celts speak a dialect called Brythonic, which is possibly derived from a language spoken as far back as the second millennium BC.

Celtic mythology is part of an oral tradition. Stories were told by travelling poets who were able to recite great tracts of the myth cycles from memory. It was not until the sixth and seventh centuries AD, in Christian times, that the Celtic myths were gathered together and written down initially by Christian monks. The great majority of Celtic myths that were collected and transcribed were Irish, mainly because the early Irish monasteries and later scribal schools were extremely prolific and highly interested in literature and its transmission. We do have some Scottish and Welsh myths, notably, in the latter case, the wonderful Mabinogi cycle of stories, but there are very few Celtic myths from mainland Europe, which is a great pity.

The fact that the Celtic myths do not come down to us from contemporary written sources, as they do in Latin and Greek mythology, but from a gathering together of spoken stories by Christian writers who had different religious beliefs, has several important consequences.

Firstly, because the myths were spoken rather than written they may have developed and mutated as they were told through the centuries or the scribes may have interpreted them differently in their writings, so many different versions of the same basic stories exist – names vary, settings change and plots differ sometimes subtly and sometimes radically. Secondly, when the myths were finally written down they were transcribed through the filter of Christianity. The Druid religion sat at the centre of Celtic life and much of the religious detail of the myths was subverted and 'Christianized' by the monks who wrote them down.

Even allowing for the Christian filter, the Celtic myths show us a culture that placed enormous value on the land, which has later been interpreted both symbolically as a veneration of a kind of 'earth mother' and practically as land being the source of life itself. Like many religions, the division between men and gods was rather blurred. Celtic gods were fallible, they made mistakes, sometimes huge ones. They could be wounded and even die. The Celtic gods were essentially men and women drawn large. In some stories they appear as mortals, in others as deities, and the whole Celtic 'pantheon' is a fluid and flexible construct – to the degree that 'god' and 'pantheon' are used here for want of more appropriate terms.

The Celts had a highly developed sense of place and their mythology confirmed this. Their myths provided the security of seeing themselves within the context of a much broader 'spiritual' reality, albeit one that was closely connected with their daily existence.

But the myths did much more than simply provide a reassuring backdrop to the Celts' often precarious existence. Certainly, it is not too difficult to see that propagandistic, political and dynastic claims underlie many of the retellings of the myths that we have recorded today. Celtic myths can be broadly split into three groups that correspond with what are described by Indo-European scholars as the 'three functions'. The First Function has to do with the basic values of the community — what is right, what is wrong, what is allowed and what is forbidden. First Function myths are concerned with how things began, who the Celts' forebears were, and where they came from. The Second Function relates to how the community protects itself and how in times of danger it defends itself. Thus Second Function myths are about idealized warriors, how they fight and how they overcome their enemies. The Third Function deals with the practical wellbeing of the community, ensuring it is well fed and safely housed. As Alexei Kondratiev talking of the Fianna puts it, 'Living on the border between culture and nature, they felt at home in both, and were bound by neither.' Third Function myths also reinforce the social importance of generosity and hospitality.

Whichever way one seeks to analyse or categorize Celtic mythology, what endures is a visceral and very human set of stories about man's relationship to his fellow man and the world they move in. Perhaps the last word on this proud, resourceful and very human people should rest with the Irish writer and broadcaster Frank Delaney: 'The Celts used their mythology, moral, heroic, magical to give themselves a history and a system for living. In myth as in life, they abundantly embraced both goodness and badness, and feared only boredom.'

Kevin Eyres

Tara to Camelot:
Celtic Place and People

A Sense of Place

In the twenty-first century, 'place' is little more than somewhere we travel to or depart from, but to the Celts place was somewhere they were rooted to and which rooted them. The span of most Celts' tangible world probably did not exceed 10 or 20 miles, and within that orbit lay everything that comprised their life. If their land produced abundant crops, harboured sufficient beasts and provided adequate fresh water, their lives were secure at least for 12 months. If their land failed them in any way, their lives were in mortal danger.

It is little wonder that, in their efforts to understand the environment that played such a pivotal role in their daily lives, the Celts gave it a magical identity and populated it with gods and goddesses bound to the very land itself.

And a Sense of Time

As important as the land and the water that ran through it was the passing of the seasons. The Celts' beliefs about the cycle of death and rebirth were reflected in their celebrations of the cycle of the seasons. The Celtic belief that death always prefigured rebirth led them to start their day with the onset of darkness and their year with the winter festival of Samhain.

The Sídhe

In the last of the great Irish invasions (the closest there is to any form of Celtic creation myth), the Irish gods, the Tuatha Dé Danann, had been banished under the ground by the Sons of Míl. Each god was given a tumulus, or mound, under which to make his home, and this is the mythical explanation for the hundreds of prehistoric mounds that cover Ireland, which are known singularly in Old Irish as the Síd and collectively as the Sídhe. They are homes to the gods, the 'ever-living ones', and so are portals to the Otherworld.

From 'The Hosting of the Sidhe'

The host is riding from Knocknarea

And over the grave of Clooth-na-Bare;

Caoilte tossing his burning hair,

And Niamh calling 'Away, come away:

Empty your heart of its mortal dream.

The winds awaken, the leaves whirl round,

Our cheeks are pale, our hair is unbound ...'

William Butler Yeats, 1893

A Holy Court

Each of the Celtic kingdoms had one place that was more important than all others. According to classical sources, every year at a preordained time the druid chief of the Carnutes of Gaul and his most senior priests met to resolve any disputes that could not be settled any other way. This was almost certainly on the site of present-day Chartres Cathedral. In Ireland, the most important political place was Tara, the seat of the kings of Ireland. In Britain, the Isle of Anglesey was the religious centre.

The Otherworld

The Celts developed one of the earliest cogent doctrines of reincarnation and immortality. The druids taught that a person's life was little more than an episode in a vast cycle of birth, death and rebirth. When a person died on earth, it merely signified that their soul had gone to another place, the Otherworld. This Otherworld, sometimes referred to as Tír na nÓg or Síd, in Ireland, was a place of feasting and home to the more major deities, who were sometimes no longer subject to the cycle of life, death and rebirth. Death for the Celts was a time of rejoicing, and the concept of the Otherworld encouraged great valour and fearlessness in their warriors.

The Kingdom of an Irish Sea God

The Irish sea god Manannán mac Lir gave his name to what we now know as the Isle of Man. Legend tells that Manannán was the first king to rule the island, holding sway over his subjects with his many magical chattels. These numbered among them a sword that could pierce any armour with ease, and an enchanted boat that could recognize and obey the thoughts of its captain. The Isle of Man has particularly strong Celtic connections, having been a Celtic-speaking culture up until a few centuries ago, and its three-legged emblem was a common design used by its craftsmen as a symbol of the island and of Mannanán – a motif evocative of the more widely used three-part designs in Celtic art.

The Royal Seat of the Kings of Ireland

Tara, in County Meath, was the royal seat of the kings of all Ireland and as such arguably the most important and sacred place in the entire isle. Time and again the Irish myths refer to Tara as not only the place where the temporal rulers reside, but also as the home of Bres and Núadu, god-kings of the Tuatha Dé Dannan reign.

The Great Celtic Festivals of the Seasons

Related to the Celtic people's deep connection to the land was their reckoning of the passage of time through sacred seasons. A poor summer or a harsh winter could spell death to the weakest and discomfort even to the strongest. Four great festivals, Samhain, Imbolc, Bealtaine and Lughnasadh, marked the turning of the seasons, and each was very different in character.

Samhain

The festival of Samhain took place around the night of 31 October and continued into the following day, 1 November, marking the start of a new year. The Coligny Calendar from first-century-BC Gaul marked the feast as Trinox Samonios. In Ireland, all fires were extinguished, to be relit by sacred flames tended by druids from the hill of Tlachtga, in County Meath. Samhain was also a festival of the dead, and those who inhabited the Otherworld returned briefly to warm themselves at the newly lit fires. The Christians adapted this important pagan festival, changing it to All Souls' Day, but something of the early Celtic feast is echoed in our celebration of Halloween.

Imbolc

The second of the great festivals that marked the seasonal cycle was Imbolc. Held on 1 February, Imbolc celebrated the end of winter and the fertile season of springtime. Imbolc also celebrated the great Irish goddess Brigid. Brigid's influence spread across healing, poetry and metalworking, all skills much valued by the Celts. Her sway in these matters was symbolized by three flaming arrows representing three fires: the fire of healing, the fire of the hearth and the fire of the smithy. Imbolc has become the feast of St Brigit in the Christian calendar and is possibly connected to the celebration of Groundhog Day in certain parts of America.

Bealtaine

The festival of Bealtaine marked the coming of summer and the time when livestock was moved out to summer pasture. One early Irish etymology suggests that 'Bealtaine' is derived from 'Bel-tinne', or the 'fires of Bel'. Bel here may be related to the continental deity Belanus, who was equated to Apollo. It was the tradition to light great bonfires on Bealtaine, and this custom survives in many places in Ireland and Scotland, where Bealtaine fires are still lit. In Scandinavian mythology, Walpurgisnacht falls on the same day as Bealtaine, and, like Bealtaine, it is celebrated with the lighting of bonfires at night. Bealtaine also commemorates the date on which the Sons of Mil arrived in Ireland.

Lughnasadh

The fourth of the great seasonal festivals of the Irish year was Lughnasadh, which celebrated the beginning of the harvest season and the ripening of the first fruits. Irish mythology tells how the great god Lug, or Lugh, first established the feast of Lughnasadh to commemorate his foster mother Tailtiu, who died clearing the

plains of Ireland so that they could be farmed. Lughnasadh was celebrated with games, horse racing and dancing, as well as with feasting. In fact, the festival is still celebrated in many parts of Ireland and by the Irish diaspora around the world. It has become a time when far-flung families traditionally gather together.

The Giant's Causeway

It is hardly surprising that when the Irish first discovered the Giant's Causeway in County Antrim, as with any other land formation they encountered, they thought that it was the work of the gods rather than the result of prehistoric volcanic action. The 40,000 regular, mostly hexagonal, basalt columns that make up this remarkable natural landmark were the subject of many myths, the most romantic being that Finn mac Cumhaill built it as a path to the Hebridean island of Staffa, home of one of his many loves.

Ben Bulben

Remarkable natural features were often incorporated into Celtic myths. This not only gave the myths more realism, but also brought the world of the gods and the world of mortals closer together. Thus it was on Ben Bulben's limestone bulk, rising spectacularly out of the Sligo plain, that Finn mac Cumhaill discovered his long-lost son Oisín wandering naked (having been born in the wild when his pregnant mother was turned into a deer). Ben Bulben was also the site of Diarmuid's death and featured in many other important myths.

Ogham

Because the Celtic myths were part of an oral rather than a written tradition, it was assumed that the Celts were largely illiterate. Then the discovery of Ogham stones in many parts of the British Isles showed that the Irish did in fact have a highly developed system of writing based around a series of straight or slanting lines. This was developed by the second century AD at the earliest and presupposes knowledge of Latin, though the majority of Ogham inscriptions are from the fourth to sixth centuries AD. The Ogham alphabet was made up of 20 letters called *fedha* that were placed above, below or through a baseline known as a *druim*. Some tales relate that Ogham was written on sticks, staves and other wooden objects, including shields.

The Origin Myth of Ogham

One legends tells how Ogma, warrior champion of the Tuatha Dé Danann and skilled in speech and poetry, developed the cipher to give a message to the god Lug about the possible abduction of his wife into the Otherworld.

The Ogham Alphabet

The Ogham alphabet's 20 letters correspond to 20 of the letters (or sounds) from our Latin alphabet as shown below:

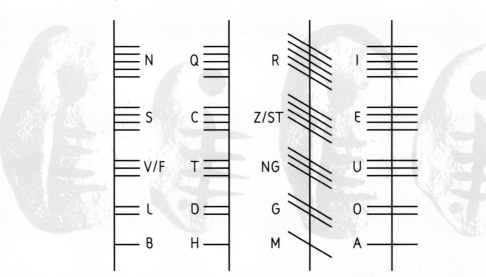

Ogham Symbolism

Each of the 20 letters of the Ogham alphabet had symbolic characteristics. Ogham was possibly seen as a magical alphabet and every letter had a bird, a colour and a tree, among various other possibilities, associated with it. Here are the first five letters of the Ogham alphabet with their corresponding symbols:

	Colour	Tree	Bird
B	White	Birch	Pheasant
L	Grey	Rowan	Duck
F	Crimson	Alder	Gull
S	'Fine-coloured'	Willow	Hawk
N	Clear	Ash	Snipe

Newgrange

Not far from Tara, the sacred seat of the high kings of Ireland, lies Newgrange, the finest prehistoric passage grave in Europe. Newgrange certainly pre-dates the Celts, but it was clearly a significant place for them. Its most common name in Irish is Brug na Bóinne, which means 'Fortress of the Boyne', the river which gets its name from the goddess Bóand. Several myths involve the site of Newgrange, one of which tells how Oengus, son of the Dagda and Bóand, tricks his father – or the cuckolded husband of Bóand, Elcmar – into allowing him to live permanently in Brug na Bóinne.

The Druids

Two distinct groups, nobles who were mostly warriors, and Druids who were the priestly class, governed the Celtic tribes. As well as acting as priests at religious ceremonies, Druids held the offices of arbitrator and magistrate, which were themselves religious functions in the ancient world. In his *Commenatrii de Bello Gallico*, Julius Caesar notes that the Druids were 'guardians of the unwritten and customary law' and as such they could pronounce sentence on wrongdoers, including exclusion from society, the ultimate sanction. Druids were not a hereditary class, and each Druid had to undergo a course of training that was both protracted and demanding.

Diodorus Siculus on Druidic Ritual

The Greek historian Diodorus Siculus, writing in the first century BC, had this to say of the Druids and their rituals:

'These men predict the future by observing the flight and calls of birds and by the sacrifice of holy animals: all orders of society are in their power ... and in very important matters they prepare a human victim, plunging a dagger into his chest; by observing the way his limbs convulse as he falls and the gushing of his blood, they are able to read the future.'

Amairgen mac Míled

In Irish mythology, Amairgen was a Son of Mil and served as a druid, poet and judge for the Milesians.

Lines from 'Amairgen's Invocation'

I invoke the spirit of Ireland,

Much-coursed be the fertile sea,

Fertile be the fruit-strewn mountains,

Fruit-strewn be the showery wood,

Showery be the river of water-falls,

Of water-falls be the lake of deep pools ...

Avalon

In Irish mythology, there are various names for the Otherworld, the earliest being Tír Tairngire ('Land of Promise'), Mag Mell ('Plain of Delights'), Tír na mBan ('Land of Women') and Emain Ablach ('Place of Apples'). Later there was Tír na nÓg ('Land of Youth'), a happy place where all was peace and harmony, and the days were spent feasting, making music and lovemaking. In later Arthurian legends, Avalon was just such a place. Arthur's mighty sword Excalibur was created by the Lady of the Lake, who may be connected to Avalon, and it was to Avalon that Arthur was taken to recover from his wounds that proved fatal. Welsh myth records a similar place to Emain Ablach called Ynys Afallach, which means 'Island of Apples' – and this is the immediate antecedent to Avalon.

Camelot

Camelot, the fabulous court of King Arthur and his Knights of the Round Table, continues to be the source of much learned controversy. Its location, if indeed it ever existed at all, was first mentioned by Chrétien de Troyes in the twelfth century. Geoffrey of Monmouth and others described Arthur's principal residence as Caerleon, a village just outside Newport in Monmouthshire. Three hundred years later, Sir Thomas Malory located it in Winchester, although his editor William Caxton disagreed with him. Cadbury Castle in Somerset, Colchester in Essex and Camelford in Cornwall have also been promoted as places where Arthur held court.

Alternative Camelots

The iconic nature of Camelot has led to the name
being used for many modern-day enterprises, including:

The presidency of John F. Kennedy in the 1960s

The operator of the UK National Lottery

A theme park in Lancashire, England

The season nine finale of the *Stargate SG-1* television series

A Japanese video game developer
(Camelot Software Planning)

A musical by Lerner and Loewe

A film (which won three Academy Awards)
starring Richard Harris as King Arthur and
Vanessa Redgrave as Guinevere

A Bloodthirsty People

'Besides some small islands round about Britain,
there is also a large island, Ierne. Concerning this
island I have nothing certain to tell, except that its
inhabitants are more savage than the Britons, since
they are man-eaters as well as heavy eaters, and
since, further, they count it an honourable thing, when
their fathers die, to devour them. But I am saying
this only with the understanding that I have no
trustworthy witnesses for it ...'

Strabo's *Geographica*, Book IV, Chapter 5 (31 BC)

Mag Mell — the Plain of Joy

Mag Mell was an Otherworld realm that was most often visited and returned from by heroes. Unlike much of the Otherworld, which was underground, Mag Mell was commonly depicted as an island that one could reach by sailing west from Ireland, though the journey would be arduous and beset with peril. As with most of the island Otherworlds, it is also referred to as the Blessed, or Fortunate, Island. Adventurers who reached Mag Mell would find a land of eternal happiness where all of life's most pleasurable activities were pursued in a place free of all sickness and death.

Annwn

In Welsh mythology, Annwn, or Annwfn, was an Otherworld literally meaning 'Un-World', a place of eternal youth and earthly delights – but also of strife according to some texts. One text, *Pwyll Pendeuic Dyfet*, has Annwn ruled over by Lord Arawn, Lord of the Otherworld, who had fierce red-eared hounds, the Cwn Annwn. Annwn was a place for the departed and the living, and could be reached by ship or would simply 'show up' in the course of one's wanderings. It was also possible to enter through a mysterious 'door' if one could discover it. Many different places have been claimed to be the location of this sacred portal, including Glastonbury Tor and Lundy Island in the Bristol Channel.

The Significance of Numbers

The Celts placed great significance on numbers and the patterns that a study of mathematics reveals. The number three was particularly important, as seen, for example, in the use of three-armed spiral, or triskele, patterns, perhaps echoing the importance of the threefold aspects and forms of gods and goddesses, and the three realms of land, sea and sky. Five was an important number in relation to the cardinal points, for example – represented by Ulster (north), Munster (south), Leinster (east) and Connaught (west), around the ancient centre of Meath.

Glastonbury

Glastonbury, a small town on the Somerset Levels, has long been associated with Celtic mythology and, later, Christian stories of the Holy Grail. Caradoc of Llancarfan says in his *Vita Gildae* in the early twelfth century that Arthur's queen, Guinevere, was abducted by Melwas and taken to Glastonbury. The tradition that Arthur and Guinevere's tomb was at Glastonbury, in the grounds of the Abbey, was first asserted by the monks of the community in 1190–91, after their monastery was destroyed by fire in 1184. A British bard then told Henry II the location of the graves; the graveyard was searched and the graves found. Then, in 1278, they were moved to a spot near the high altar in the abbey church, but were then destroyed in the sixteenth century with the dissolution of the monasteries under Henry VIII.

The Dindshenchas

Celtic mythology, like any folklore tradition, is much concerned with explaining how things came to be as they are. The dindshenchas are relatively short Irish poems or prose narratives that illustrate how places received their names. Dindshenchas lore can be found collected in The Book of Leinster manuscript, as well as within the larger Irish prose tales, including *Táin Bó Cúailnge* and *Acallam na Senórach*.

Temair Breg, cid ní diatá?

This dindshenchas begins to tell the story of how Tara,
the most revered of all Irish sites, received its name.

Temair Breg, whence is it named?

declare O sages!

when did the name part from the stead?

when did Temair become Temair?

Was it under Partholan of the battles?

or at the first conquest by Cesair?

or under Nemed of the fresh valour?

or under Cigal of the knocking knees?

Was it under the Firbolgs of the boats?

or from the line of the Lupracans?

tell which conquest of these it was

from which the name Temair was set on Temair?

More words from 'Temair Breg, cid ní diatá':

The Seat of the Kings was its name:

the kingly line of the Milesians reigned in it:

five names accordingly were given it

from the time when it was Fordruim till it was Temair.

I am Fintan the poet,

I am a salmon not of one stream;

it is there I was exalted with fame,

on the sod-built stead, even Temair.

Standing Stones and Stone Circles

Most prehistoric standing stones and stone circles such as Stonehenge in Wiltshire and Carnac in Brittany (where an incredible 3,000 prehistoric stones were hewn out of local rock and erected in perfect straight lines) pre-date the Celts. There is little doubt, however, that the Celts would have reckoned them important landmarks, and their holy men, the Druids, may have adopted many of these magical places and used them for their own ceremonies and forms of worship.

Sacred Water

The Celts held a special reverence for water in all its forms.
In common with other peoples of Indo-European origin, they
attached great symbolic importance to rivers. Indeed many of
the great rivers of Europe still have names that reflect Celtic origins.
For example, the Danube's name (Danuvius) is related to the Irish
goddess Danu (and arguably so is the Rhone's with Rhodanus).
In Hindu mythology, there is also a goddess called Danu
and the name means 'waters of heaven' in Sanskrit.

Portals to the Otherworld

Celts habitually made offerings to water gods by throwing objects of value into rivers, pools and wells. King Arthur received his mighty sword Excalibur from the Lady of the Lake, and it was to her lake that he had it returned as he lay dying.

As well as leaving votive offerings in water, the Celts may have buried their great heroes by leaving their bodies in rivers. Indeed the Thames, originally the Tamesis, possibly meaning 'dark river', was thought by the Celts to be a portal to the Otherworld.

Giants on Hillsides

Three great figures cut into the chalk hills of the south of England may well owe their origins to the Celts. Although there is some dispute about the actual date of their original carving, the Cerne Abbas Giant in Dorset, the Long Man of Wilmington in East Sussex and the wonderfully elegant White Horse of Uffington on the Ridgeway in Oxfordshire may all be gigantic representations of Celtic gods. This is art on a truly epic scale. As a depiction of the human figure, only the Inca Giant of the Atacama Desert in Chile exceeds The Long Man of Wilmington in size.

I am wind which breathes upon the sea,

I am wave of the ocean,

I am murmur of the billows,

I am stag of the seven combats,

I am hawk upon the rocks,

I am a beam of the sun,

I am the fairest of plants,

I am a wild boar in valour,

I am a salmon in the water,

I am a lake in the plain,

I am the excellence of arts,

I am the point of the spear of battle,

I am the god who forms subjects for a ruler.

From *The Mystery of Amairgen*, Amairgen, son of Mil

A Sprawling Collection:
Gods, Goddesses, Heroes and Heroines

Celtic Deities

The various Celtic cultures had a huge sprawling collection of deities, some universally acknowledged, others very much *geni loci*, local gods attached to a particular place, river or geographic feature. There was never a definitive catalogue of deities because the Celtic cultures were so varied and often so far removed from each other that standardization and universalization were neither possible nor desirable. Furthermore, as the Celts were a loose confederation of tribes rather than a homogenous group, each region had its own gods, or where it had gods in common with other Celtic groupings the names they gave the gods often changed. Even the relationship of one god to another could vary fundamentally from region to region.

Irish Gods and Goddesses

As with nearly all aspects of Celtic mythology, it is the gods of the Irish that we know most about. Even here it is impossible to be definitive about the relationship of one deity to another, but what we can say is that the vast majority of Irish gods were Tuatha Dé Danann, 'People/Tribes of the Gods of Danu', who settled in Ireland before the coming of the Milesians. Many of the Tuatha Dé Danann had mortal as well as divine qualities – a common feature of Celtic mythological characters.

Danu

Danu (or Dana) is often described today as the Irish earth mother or goddess of fertility, though in fact there is no real evidence for this role as there are no narratives concerning her. However, the territorial goddess Anu, might be related to or have had her characteristics applied to Danu. 'Mother' or at least eponymous ancestor of the Tuatha Dé Danann dynasty, she has cognates in other Celtic cultures, including Dôn in Wales. The possible union of Danu with, Tuirill Bicreo (or Delbáeth), who was her father and was a son of Ogma, gave birth to Brian, Iuchar, and Iucharba, who went on to kill Lug's father and embark upon many adventures to repay Lug for this offense.

Núadu

The son of Echtach, Núadu commanded the Tuatha Dé Danann's battle with the Fir Bolg. Núadu has the epithet of Airgetlám, 'Silver Hand', because in the first great battle of Moytura his hand was severed by a Fir Bolg warrior, and the physician Dian Cécht replaced his hand with a working one fashioned from silver by the artificer god Crédne. Núadu was the grandfather of the legendary Finn mac Cumhaill, known in Anglicized form as Finn McCool. Núadu's Romano-British cognate is Nodons, a deity associated with the healing spring at Lydney Park, Gloucestershire.

103

Lug

Lug, or Lugh is another god of confusing parentage, who is said to be the son of Ethliu, or Eithne, who is the daughter of the Fomorian Balor; his father is usually Cian, who is a son of Dian Cécht, although alternate paternal grandfathers are sometimes given, and later folklore gives Cian a different name altogether. He is commonly called Lámfhota, 'long hand', a reference to his skill with a sling, and Samildánach, 'skilled in all the arts'. A popular and widespread pan-Celtic deity, he appears in the mythology of the Continental Celts as Lugus and in Wales, where he is called Lleu Llaw Gyffes, 'Lleu of the Skilful Hand'.

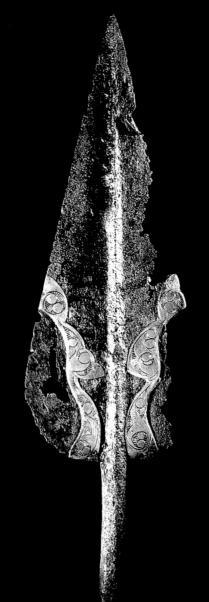

Lug's Hound

Lug had many enchanted weapons, including a ferocious living spear, so dangerous that it had to be kept in a cauldron of water to suppress its fiery heat from burning all things around it when not in use. Lug also had a magical hound named Fáilinis, which the Fianna warrior and poet Caílte described thus:

That hound of mightiest deeds,

Which was irresistible in hardness of combat,

Was better than wealth ever known,

A ball of fire every night.

Other virtues had that beautiful hound

(Better this property than any other property),

Mead or wine would grow of it,

Should it bathe in spring water.

The Dagda

The Dagda, whose name means 'good god' (in the sense of being good at things, not morally good), is usually said to have been fathered by Elatha, and in one source his mother is Ethliu (or Eithne), the Fomorian mother of Lug. The Dagda was leader of the Tuatha Dé Danann after Lug. A character of superhuman strength and appetite, he famously devoured a deep pit of porridge using a ladle so large that a man and woman could sleep in it. The Dagda is connected with several mythical objects, including a cauldron of food that is never empty, a club that can both kill and give life, and a harp that could cause laughing, weeping and sleeping. The Dagda appears to have been mainly an Irish deity, though there is a possibly similar figure in the Gaulish Sucellos, the hammer god and 'good striker'.

Ogma

Ogma, warrior champion of the Tuatha Dé Danann and god of eloquence, is a son of Elatha (possibly a different Elatha than the Fomorian father of Bres) and a brother of the Dagda; his mother is sometimes stated to be Eithliu, the mother of Lug. Ogma gave his name to Ogham, the ancient Irish alphabet used by the Druids. Ogmios, a Gaulish god of eloquence who was also given Hercules' attributes, and who trailed a retinue of men attached with chains to his tongue, seems to be a similar figure.

Threefold Goddesses

In Celtic mythology, female deities could be as visceral and bloodthirsty as their male counterparts. They often took the form of tripartite or triple goddesses, whereby they were connected to three different aspects or took on three different forms (and here we do not mean in the sense of maiden-mother-crone). This sovereignty over more than one realm made them powerful adversaries and valuable allies. Like the male deities, the goddesses were prey to many mortal foibles. They could be jealous, vengeful and malicious, and were liable to support first one side, then the other, in battle. It is interesting to note that there is no readily identifiable goddess of love in the Celtic pantheon (although really there is no 'god/goddess of X' in anything Celtic — often several gods at a time are connected to something, be it healing or poetry, for example).

The Morrígan

The most formidable of the tripartite goddesses was the Morrígan. In her own right or in one of her three aspects — Nemain, Badb and Macha, sometimes said to be a collective group called the Morrígan, within which there is often variation — she was a fearful presence on the battlefield, inciting soldiers, attacking warriors in her animal forms as scaldcrow, eel, heifer or wolf, and scavenging among the dead of battle. Illustrative of her typical behaviour was her part in the story of Cú Chulainn, whom she first attempted to seduce, and then, when she was rejected, did everything in her power to destroy. Her figure may have influenced the portrayal of the Arthurian character Morgan le Fay, the sorceress and adversary of King Arthur, her half brother.

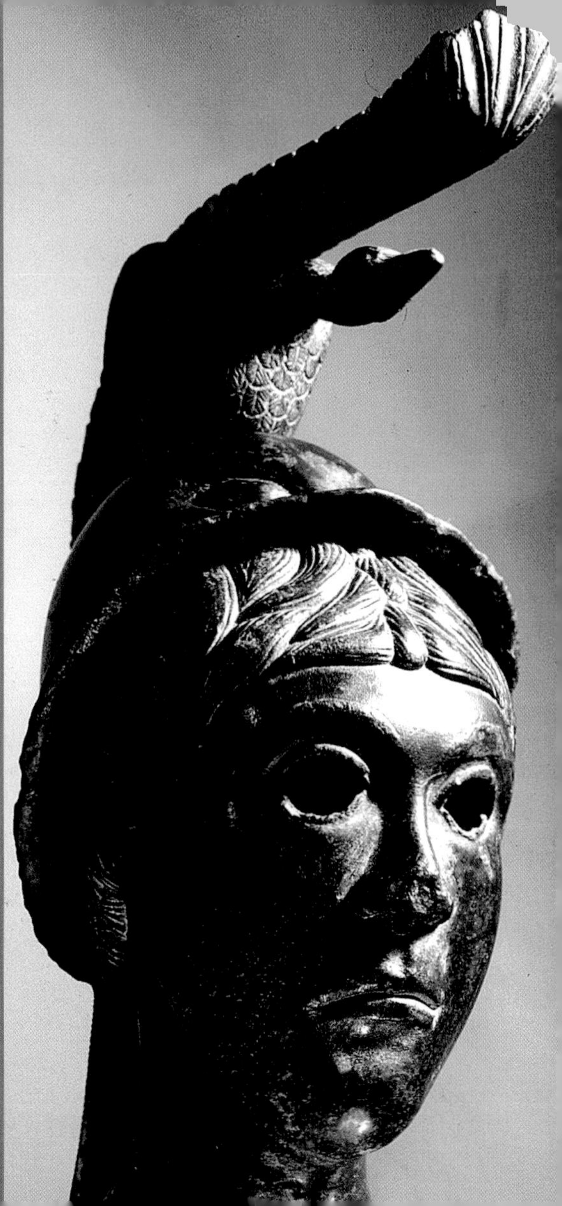

Brigid

Brigid (or Brigit), 'the exalted one', is a more benign presence. Along with her two sisters, also called Brigid (who could be considered as no more than other facets of Brigid's personality), she was the daughter of the Dagda. Brigid was a warrior goddess, but was also patron of the arts of poetry, healing and smithcraft. Deities of the arts and crafts of metalworking were highly esteemed in a society which valued the artistic and practical applications of metalwork for ornament as well as for military technology.

Triple Deities in Other Mythologies

The concept of the threefold deity is not, of course, exclusively Celtic.

The Christian religion is founded on the Holy Trinity – God the Father,

God the Son and God the Holy Ghost. Other triple deities include:

The Three Pure Ones of Taoism

The three aspects of god in Hinduism – Vishnu, Brahma and Shiva

The three Fates of Greece – the Spinner,

the Measurer and the Cutter of the Thread of Life

The Three Norns, or Weird Sisters, of Norse mythology

The One, the Thought (Intellect) and the Soul of Neoplatonic philosophy

Jung on Threefold Deities

'Triads of gods appear very early, at the primitive
level. The archaic triads in the religions of antiquity and
of the East are too numerous to be mentioned here.
Arrangement in triads is an archetype in the history
of religion, which in all probability formed the basis
of the Christian Trinity.'

Carl Jung, *A Psychological Approach to the Dogma of the Trinity*

Epona

Epona, the Great Mare, was the Continental Celtic horse goddess. Her name contains the same roots from which we derive the English word 'pony'. As with most Celtic deities, she had complex spheres of influence, including healing, fertility and possibly even the safeguarding of the human soul. Epona is unique in being the only Celtic goddess to be assimilated fully into the Roman pantheon, having a temple in her honour in Rome along with the feast date of 18 December.

Manannán mac Lir

Although he pre-dates the Tuatha Dé Danann, Manannán, mac Lir, which means 'son of the sea', is generally considered as one of their number. Manannán, like Epona, was a psychopomp, or 'guide of souls', but he was also the protector of the Blessed Isles and the ruler of Mag Mell. Among his magical possessions he has a colour-shifting cloak and is often portrayed as riding the waves on an ornately decorated chariot. In Wales his equivalent is Manawydan ap Llyr, who married Rhiannon after the death of Pwyll, chief of Dyfed.

Magical Beasts

Celtic gods often took on the form of animals, and when they did so they took on the characteristics of the particular animal or bird. Beasts such as boar were highly prized not just for their meat, but also because of their behaviour in the hunt, and regularly appear as divine beings both in the natural realm and the Otherworlds. The boar at bay was often cited as the exemplary image of how warriors should behave in battle. The stag was also an important beast, associated with Cernunnos, a Gaulish horned god, and with other similar horned figures (perhaps gods of fertility and wealth) that were depicted throughout the Celtic world.

And Miraculous Birds

The Celts also revered birds and we can see from their art, especially from their exquisite brooches and statuary, that they had a profound knowledge and affection for all winged creatures. Indeed, images of birds appear on ritual vessels as far back as the Hallstatt period (*c.* 700–500 BC). Both humans and gods took the form of swans, and a gold chain around the bird's neck sometimes signified these transformations, though often it would simply represent the bird's otherworldliness. In an Irish legend, the four children of Lir were transformed into swans by Aoife, their evil stepmother.

The Influence of the Gods

The deities of Celtic mythology impacted on the lives of all of the great Celtic heroes. There were three principal ways that gods and goddesses influenced mortal lives. First, they could, and frequently did, curse both individuals and whole tribes: the goddess Macha cursed the men of Ulster so that they were as weak in battle as if they were 'women in labour'. Secondly, they could prophesy and so predetermine the future. Thirdly, they could 'shape shift' into animal or alternate human forms at will.

Shape Shifters

In today's mythologies, science fiction and fantasy, creatures constantly change their shape and characteristics. In Celtic mythology, shape shifting was a commonplace event. The Morrígan changed form no fewer than three times when she attacked Cú Chulainn at the ford during his battle with Lóch mac Emonis. The Celtic fascination with the way things can change their appearance, their physical attributes and their very nature is borne out in their art. Both in their metalworking and later in their illumination of manuscripts, Celtic craftsmen fashioned designs that at first sight may seem abstract, but on closer investigation reveal the form of an animal or human.

A Sprawling Collection: Gods, Goddesses, Heroes and Heroines

Human Shape Shifting

It was not only deities who were capable of shape shifting. The truly great human heroes of Celtic mythology also often underwent profound physical changes in various circumstances, including in the heat of battle. This was most remarkable in the case of Cú Chulainn, as the following passage from the *Táin Bó Cúailnge* (*Cattle Raid of Cooley*) graphically conveys.

Cú Chulainn
Prepares for Battle

When all was made ready, Cú Chulainn felt a series of great spasms shake his body. His face itself turned into a hideous mask of raw throbbing flesh, with one eye sunken far into his skull and the other dangling loose from its socket. Cú Chulainn's hair hissed and curled like a nest of serpents and his lips curled back till his whole jaw and gullet were clearly visible. A blinding light shone from his brow and sprays of ink-black blood gushed from the crown of his head. Thus did Cú Chulainn go out to face his enemy.

From *Táin Bó Cúailnge (Cattle Raid of Cooley)*

Welsh Deities

The Welsh had their own extensive pantheon. Some gods and goddesses, such as Llyr and Don (who really are simply names in genealogies with very little narrative or description to go with them), were the cognates of Irish gods or goddesses, but others were specifically Welsh or, as in the case of Rhiannon, had a very different story in comparison to similar figures in Irish mythology.

The Houses of Don and Llyr

The families descended from Don (cognate to Danu in Ireland) and Llyr (cognate to Lir in Ireland) are referred to as the Children of Don and the Children of Llyr. The complex history of their conflict is told in the Four Branches of the *Mabinogi*, with the Children of Don's story taking place in North Wales, while that of the Children of Llyr (who include Bendigeidfran, Branwen and Manawydan) takes place in Mid Wales.

Aranrhod

One of the children of Don, Aranrhod's name may mean 'silver wheel', and the constellation Corona Borealis was associated with her fortress, Caer Aranrhod. In the Fourth Branch of the *Mabinogi*, she is summoned by her uncle Math to be his virgin footholder on the advice of her brother Gwydion, but she fails the test of her virginity by giving birth to a son, Dylan Eil Ton ('sea, son of wave'), and a 'small creature' which later matured into Lleu Llaw Gyffes. Dylan took to the sea immediately, but was later slain by his uncle Gofannon, a smith deity.

Aranrhod swore that Lleu would never have a name, arms or a wife that was of the human race, but her clever brother Gwydion tricked her into granting the first two rights to her son.

Lleu Llaw Gyffes

One of several Welsh cognates to the Irish god Lug, Lleu Llaw Gyffes earned his name ('fair-haired one of the skilful hand') when, while disguised as a shoemaker, he hit a wren on its leg between the tendon and the bone with a needle. The Continental Celtic Lugoves were deities of shoemakers, and Lleu Llaw Gyffes was considered one of the 'three golden shoemakers' in the Welsh Triads, thus a relationship between all of these figures seems likely.

After his mother Aranrhod's attempts to foil Lleu's destiny, the woman Blodeuedd was created as his wife by Gwydion and Math. Blodeuedd took a lover, and the two attempted to kill Lleu, succeeding only in transforming him into an eagle, whose flesh slowly rotted in a forest hideaway. Gwydion eventually found the eagle, charmed it down with poetry, and turned Lleu back to his original form. The lover of his wife was killed, and Blodeuedd was turned into an owl as punishment.

Arawn, King of Annwn

Arawn, the king of Annwn, the Otherworld, was a central character in the first branch of the *Mabinogi*, the great Welsh myth cycle. One day, when Arawn and Pwyll, lord of Dyfed, were seeking the same stag, Pwyll set his hounds on the downed animal despite Arawn's hounds having killed it first, driving off Arawn's pack. In order to repay Arawn for this offense, Pwyll changed places with him for a year and a day. During this time they were so well disguised that no one realized the deception, not even Arawn's beautiful wife. Pwyll never once made love to Arawn's wife, and also managed to vanquish Hafgan, Arawn's enemy, and as a result he became Arawn's close friend and ally.

Rhiannon

Although mortal, Rhiannon apparently comes from the Otherworld, has otherworldly birds and spends a great deal of time trapped in the Otherworld. Her name means 'Great Queen' (therefore making her very similar to the Morrígan), and she seems to be the Welsh reflex of the horse goddess, having similarities with Epona, the great horse goddess. A superhuman horsewoman, Rhiannon easily outran the fastest horses of Pwyll of Dyfed.

As the daughter of Hefeydd the Old, she certainly had magical powers, but some might interpret her as preferring to ignore them and cope with what fate dealt her as a human. Her refusal to rebut the false claims of infanticide brought against her led to her spending seven years excluded from court. Rhiannon experiences much strife in the tales of the *Mabinogi*.

Spirits
The Mysterious Genii Cucullati

The *geni cucullati,* or hooded spirits, appear in sculptures and carvings across regions

inhabited by Celtic peoples, from the British Isles to the Rhine. It is assumed that these

figures are spirits that are in some way connected with fertility, but they have no names

and are of indeterminate sex, although statues found in the Moselle region do

sometimes wear moustaches. These hooded spirits vary in size from large and upright to small and stooping. Uniquely in Britain, where they have been found as far north as Hadrian's Wall and as far south as Gloucester, they generally appear in groups of three, leading to speculation that they could represent another example of a tripartite deity.

The Mischievous Pooka

Another example of a shape-shifting spirit was the impish pooka (Anglicized from the Irish púca), who has been variously described as a malevolent force in the guise of a horse that offered dangerous rides to credulous travellers, a synonym for the devil, or alternatively a benevolent creature generally fond of the company of humans.

Impish Spirits from Six European Regions

The Púca from Ireland

The Pwca from Wales

Bucca from Cornwall

Puck from England

Pukki from Scandinavia

The Pouque from the Channel Islands

The Romano-Celtic Pantheon

Virtually all of the Celtic deities from Britain and mainland Europe

come from the Romano-Celtic period, the time when the Romans

were at least nominally in charge. The Romans adopted some of the

Celtic deities, adapted others and sometimes simply gave them the

name of the nearest equivalent Roman god. After the legalization

of Christianity by Constantine I at the beginning of the fourth

century AD, many of the Celtic gods became absorbed

into this new pervasive religion as saints.

Seven Romano-British Gods

Agroná – goddess of battle and slaughter

Brigantia – foremost, the tutelary goddess (one acting as protector or guardian) of the tribe of the Brigantes; connected to water, and syncretized to Minerva by the Romans

Belatucadros – syncretized to Mars, so possbly a god of war (Mars also had an agricultural function)

Britannia – the tutelary goddess of Britain

Coventina – nymph-like goddess of a healing well at Carrawburgh on Hadrian's Wall, and so sometimes referred to as a goddess of rivers and springs

Maponus – god of music and poetry syncretized to Apollo

Sulis – goddess of the healing springs at Bath, which were originally called *Aquae Sulis* in Latin

And Seven Romano-Gaulish Gods

Ancamna – mother or healing goddess of the Treveri; consort of Mars

Andarte – goddess of victory; connected to bears

Borvo – god of healing springs

Lugus – connected with youth and shoemaking, and the cognate of Lug; (often misinterpreted as the god of light)

Nantosvelta – possible patroness of home and hearth, whose name means 'winding river'; consort of Sucellos; also connected to ravens

Rigisamus – syncretized to Mars (but hard to be sure in what capacity, so possibly a god of war)

Heroes

Heroes of Celtic mythology reflect the core Celtic values: great courage in battle, a knowledge and love of literature, and an understanding of magic and the ways of the Otherworld. Celtic heroes, like their gods, are by no means perfect. They can suffer unreasonable jealousy, harbour irrational grudges and be prey to fantastic rages which render them incapable of distinguishing friend from foe. At times Celtic heroes almost cross the boundary between human and god, but whatever they do they never lose their essential humanity and fallibility.

Conn Cétchathach

Conn Cétchathach (Conn of the Hundred Battles) was one of the earliest of the high kings of Ireland and one of many who ruled at Tara. He gained his epithet during the bloody battles he fought with the Dál nAraidi, a kingdom of Ulster. After his declaration as king by the Lia Fáil, the Stone of Destiny at Tara, Conn founded a dynasty that endured for several centuries.

Cormac mac Airt

The illustrious Cormac mac Airt, one of the most legendary of high kings of Ireland, was the grandson on Conn Cétchathach. His rule was placed during the same legendary time period of most of the Fenian cycle tales, and he made use of the services of Finn mac Cumhaill and his Fianna warriors on several occasions.

As a king, Cormac was famous for the wisdom and evenhandedness of his judgements and, in the seventeenth-century *Annals of Clonmacnoise*, he is described as 'the best king that ever raigned (*sic*) in Ireland' (in comparison to those that reigned before him).

Cú Chulainn

Cú Chulainn was a truly magnificent figure who strode across the early Irish myth cycles leaving a trail of death and devastation in his wake. Cú Chulainn, often referred to as the Hound of Ulster, is the central character in the great *Táin Bó Cúailnge* (*Cattle Raid of Cooley*), where he single-handedly defended Ulster from the forces of Connacht (and the attacks of the supernatural Morrígan, whose advances he had earlier spurned). Before going into battle he could summon up a tremendous fury that would transform him into a truly invincible warrior no matter what the odds.

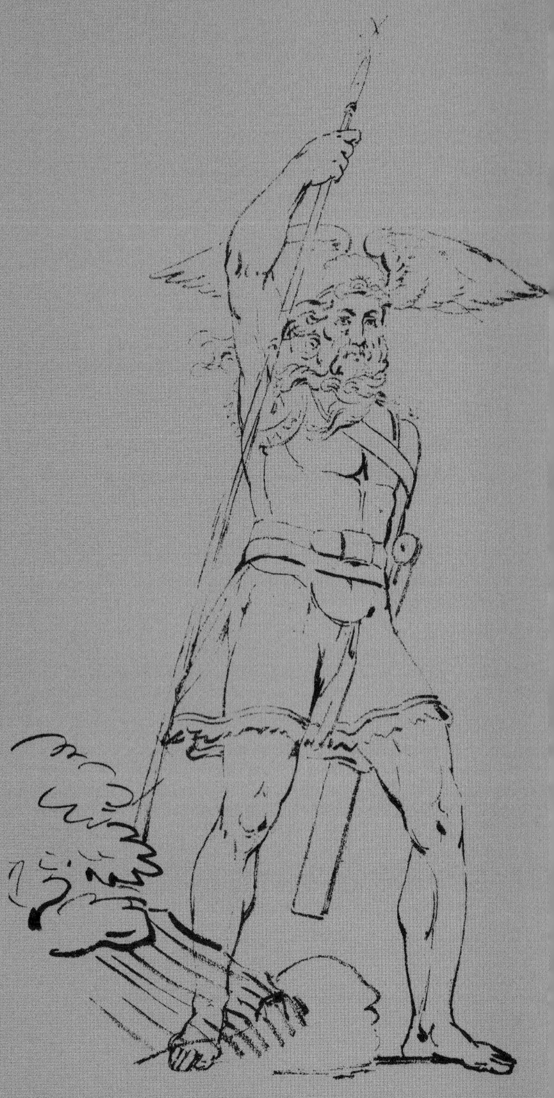

Finn mac Cumhaill

Where Cú Chulainn was a solitary figure preferring to fight single-handed, Finn (or Fionn in Modern Irish) mac Cumhaill was a leader, marshalling his band of warriors, the Fianna, and deciding who they should assist and who they should attack. Like Cú Chulainn, Finn had studied poetry, literature and music as well as the arts of warfare and, having eaten the Salmon of Wisdom, he had the gift of foresight and divine knowledge. Despite this and his courage in battle however, he showed a less admirable facet of his character in his old age when he pursued a bitter vendetta against his former comrade Diarmuid.

Diarmuid Ua Duibhne

Diarmuid Ua Duibhne was one of the greatest warriors of Finn mac Cumhaill's Fianna, and one of Finn's most valued lieutenants. Although a courageous fighter and a skilled huntsman, he is chiefly remembered as a lover. Dairmuid had been given a 'love-spot' as a young man, and this made him irresistible to women. He used this gift honourably, however, and when Gráinne, who was betrothed to his lord, Finn, attempted to seduce him he resisted. It was Gráinne's use of a *geis* (or supernatural injunction) that led to their elopement and the subsequent enduring attempts of Finn to gain revenge. Diarmuid died as honourably as he had lived, struck down by Finn, his former lord and comrade.

Oisín

Last of the great Fenian heroes, Oisín was the son of Finn mac Cumhaill, and the progeny of Finn's tragic marriage to his great love Sadb, who took the form of a deer. Oisín spent the early years of his life as a feral child, until Finn found him wandering naked on Ben Bulben. Once reunited with his father, Oisín quickly became an accomplished poet and an expert swordsman. He left the Fianna, spirited to the mythical Tír na nÓg ('Land of Youth') by the Otherworld woman Niamh. In later legends, Oisín returns from Tír na nÓg 300 earth years later when he meets and debates with Saint Patrick, patron saint of Ireland.

The Wanderings of Oisin

Caoilte, and Conan, and Finn were there,

When we followed a deer with our baying hounds.

With Bran, Sceolan, and Lomair,

And passing the Firbolgs' burial-mounds,

Came to the cairn-heaped grassy hill

Where passionate Maeve is stony-still;

And found On the dove-grey edge of the sea

A pearl-pale, high-born lady, who rode

On a horse with bridle of findrinny;

And like a sunset were her lips,

A stormy sunset on doomed ships.

Extract from *The Wanderings of Oisin*, William Butler Yeats

An Eighteenth-Century Fraud?

In 1760 a Scottish poet, James Macpherson, published an epic saga in verse form called *Ossian*. He claimed this was a direct translation of an ancient third-century Scottish manuscript he had discovered. Although *Ossian* proved popular, academics including Samuel Johnson questioned the authenticity of the work, claiming that Macpherson had in fact woven the story around some fragments of an ancient story, most of the content being his own. Although Macpherson strongly disputed these claims, he never produced the original documents.

Pronouncing Celtic Names

Pronunciation of Irish and Welsh names might appear difficult from an English speaker's perspective. Here are some phonetic versions of Insular Celtic names:

Cú Chulainn – Koo Hoolan (make the 'h' sound more of a harsh, glottal sound, like the German Ba<u>ch</u>)

Gráinne – GRA-nyeh

Diarmuid – JUR-muhd (because the initial 'd' is slender)

Finn mac Cumhaill – Finn mack KUV-all

Niamh – NEE-uv

sídhe – she

Oisín – OSH-een

Táin Bó Cúailnge – TOYN Bow COOL-in-ya

Medb – METH-uv

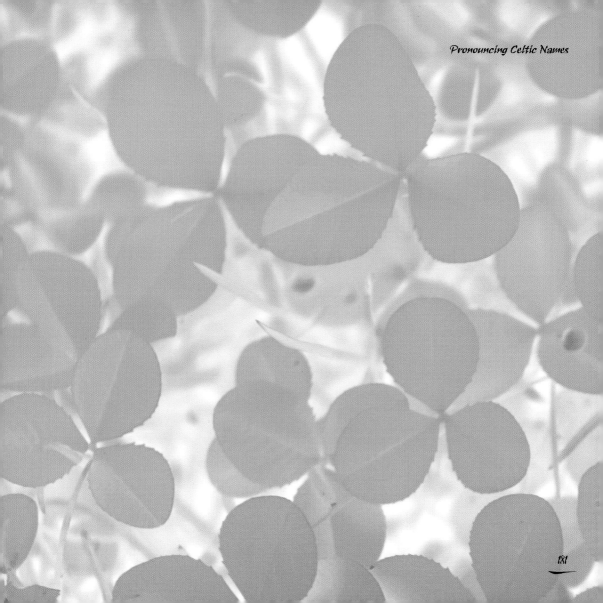

King Arthur

Best known of all the Celtic heroes is King Arthur, who with his Knights of the Round Table brought peace and prosperity to a troubled England. Although Arthur is familiar to most readers from the medieval romances of Chrétien de Troyes, Geoffrey of Monmouth and Sir Thomas Malory, Arthur emerges as a character in Welsh historical works of the ninth century, as well as Welsh prose and poetic narratives from the tenth to the twelfth centuries. Arthur, son of King Uther Pendragon, was brought up away from his father's court with no knowledge of his royal parentage. By pulling the sword from the stone, he proved his right to be king of England, and from his fabulous court at Camelot he ruled over his people wisely and well.

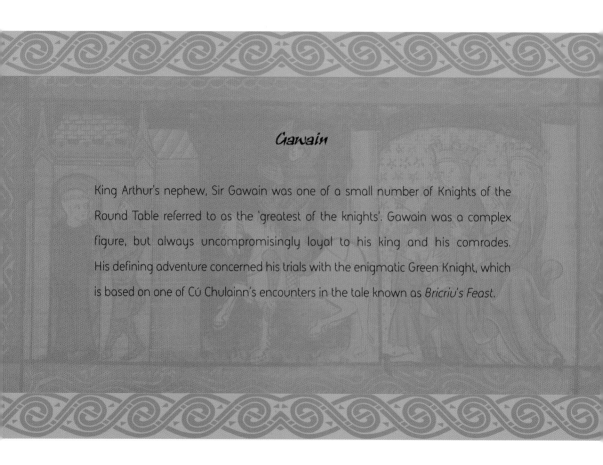

Gawain

King Arthur's nephew, Sir Gawain was one of a small number of Knights of the Round Table referred to as the 'greatest of the knights'. Gawain was a complex figure, but always uncompromisingly loyal to his king and his comrades. His defining adventure concerned his trials with the enigmatic Green Knight, which is based on one of Cú Chulainn's encounters in the tale known as *Bricriu's Feast*.

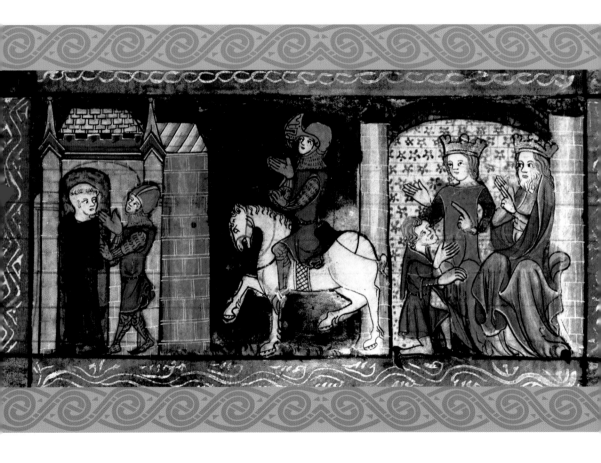

Lancelot

Of all Arthur's faithful knights, Lancelot was the greatest and most trusted. Lancelot, or Galahad as he is sometimes known, was himself a king, being the son of King Ban of Benoic, but according to some accounts he is not aware of his lineage or indeed who his parents were. Lancelot was a formidable warrior and a tireless fighter for Arthur's cause; however he fell fatally and incontrovertibly in love with Guinevere, Arthur's queen. It was Lancelot's tragic love for Guinevere that finally destroyed the court at Camelot and brought about Arthur's eventual downfall.

Pronouncing Celtic Names

Rhiannon – hree-AN-un

Pwyll – POO-ul (the closest one can get without pronouncing the proper Welsh double 'l')

Hefeydd – HEV-eth

Núadu – NOO-a-thoo

Lug – Loog

Caílte mac Ronáin – KWIL-chuh mac Ronan

Tuatha Dé Danann – TOO-uh-thuh DAY DAN-an

Donn – Don

Dagda – DOG-da

Villains and Monsters

The concept of intrinsic villainy is problematic when it comes to any Celtic narrative, as many gods and heroes had their 'villainous' sides (not unlike many other religions and mythologies): the Morrígan was a rather terrifying figure; Finn himself was in the role of the villain with Diarmuid; Cú Chulainn was sometimes a greater danger to his own people than his enemies; and Gwydion is one of the main heroes of the Fourth Branch of the *Mabinogi*, and yet he also brings about the death of Pryderi, one of the heroes of the first three branches. Even the Fomorians, who are often seen as wholly evil (which would make Lug at least half intrinsically evil), are spoken about in the oldest Irish poems in terms similar to the Tuatha Dé Danann. Still, some characters of Celtic mythology can certainly be said to be more evil and monstrous than others ...

The Fomorians

The aboriginal inhabitants of Ireland, the Fomorians, a race of formidable giants, were a constant threat to the early civilizing invaders. Some Fomorians are described in certain accounts as having the head of a goat and the body of a man, though there is some dispute in the sources over whether the Gobarchinn ('goat-heads') are a separate race, as there are other races of animal-headed beings described in various parts of Irish literature. Some Fomorians might have only one eye; others have no heads, and mouths in their chests; while still others, such as Bres and Elatha and Indech, seem to be for all intents and purposes completely 'human' in shape and form, and lack of disability. In spite of this, the Fomorians were formidable fighters. Some Fomorians could be noble and fair, and this led to a certain amount of intermarrying between the Fomorians and their foes.

A Sprawling Collection: Gods, Goddesses, Heroes and Heroines

Balor

Most terrible of all the Fomorians was Balor of the Evil Eye. Balor's eye would immediately kill anyone its gaze fell upon. In battle this eye, which was normally kept closed, was raised by a team of four men using a 'polished ring' attached to his eyelid. In the final great battle between the Tuatha Dé Danann and the Fomorians, Balor kills their leader Núadu, but is in turn killed by a sling shot from Lug.

Goll mac Morna

A recurrent theme of the Fenian Cycle is concerned with the feud between the Clan Baiscne and the Clan Morna over the right to claim to be the true Fenians. The Clan Morna are the villains of the piece, and none is more villainous than Goll mac Morna, the one-eyed clan leader. Goll killed Finn mac Cumhaill's father Cumhaill, whom he beheaded. To compound the deed, Goll then made off not only with Cumhaill's head, but also with all his possessions, leaving Cumhaill's wife, Muirne, destitute and pregnant with Finn.

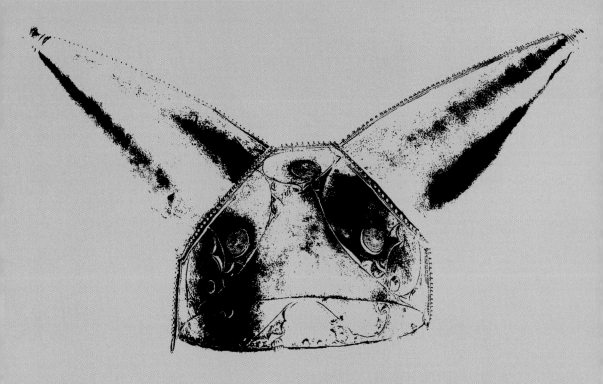

Conán mac Morna

Unusually in Celtic mythology, Conán mac Morna is often a comical character, who might almost have come out of a modern Asterix tale. He is more of a troublemaker than a villain, as in most Fenian texts he's on Finn's side. Conán, often called Conán the Bald, was a fat, unattractive character and the brother of Goll, leader of the Clan Morna. He was renowned for his continual complaining and his impetuousity – he never ran from a fight.

Dullahan

Dullahan (the Dark Man) was a headless creature usually pictured riding a headless horse with his own head under his arm. Dullahan may have been connected to the spirit of the fierce Irish god Crom Dubh, who apparently demanded annual human sacrifices from his followers and to have been worshipped in Ireland until the fifth century AD, when St Patrick was said to have destroyed his idols and abolished the practice.

Asterix

It would be churlish not to mention that great Gallic Celt and thorn in the side of the Roman invaders of his country, Asterix the Gaul. Through the pages of the 33 main comic books (translated into more than a hundred languages) and innumerable spin-offs, Asterix, his long-suffering friend and ally Obelix, and the irascible Druid Getafix have tirelessly made fools of the occupying Roman Legions and poked fun at just about every other European nation.

Battles, Voyages and Romance: The Myths

The Creation Myths – The Book of Invasions

The earliest Irish myths that we know of – in terms of legendary history – concern the prehistory of Ireland. These stories were collected together by Irish scholars from the eighth to the twelfth centuries and were given the collective title of *Lebor Gabála Érenn* – meaning the 'Book of the Takings of Ireland'. It is more commonly known in English as 'The Book of Invasions' and describes the invasions of Ireland that culminated in the arrival of the Gaels, destined to rule Ireland for posterity.

Cesair

The Book of Invasions begins with the coming of Cesair, daughter of Bith, the son of Noe (Noah) before the Flood. Cesair brought with her three men, Bith, Fintan and Ladra, and 50 women. The women were shared out between the men with the intention of populating the island. However, Ladra and then Bith died, leaving Fintan to flee under the pressure. The rest of Cesair's people were wiped out in the Flood, and only Fintan survived, turning into a salmon.

Partholon's People

Three hundred years after the Flood, Partholon settled in Ireland with his three sons and their people. After 10 years of peace, however, war broke out with the aboriginal people of Ireland – a tribe of monstrous creatures called the Fomorians. Although the Partholonians were victorious, this victory was short-lived, as after clearing four plains and creating seven lakes, they were wiped out by plague in a single week. They are said to have been buried on the Old Plain of Elta to the southwest of Dublin, in an area that is still called Tallaght, which means 'plague grave'.

The Conquest of Nemed

When Nemed, a Scythian warrior, arrived in Ireland, it had been laid waste by the series of terrible plagues. Of a fleet of more than 30 boats, only Nemed's survived; the rest sank in the waters of the Caspian Sea.

Nemed conquered and enslaved the Fomorians, but after his death they rose up and in turn enslaved the Children of Nemed, forcing them to agree to a terrible annual tribute of two-thirds of their corn and two-thirds of their children.

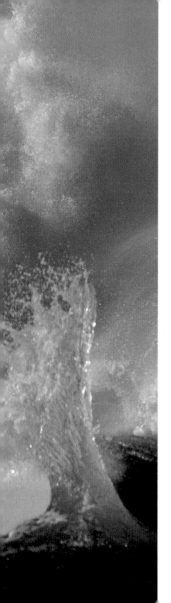

The Invasion of the Children of Nemed

The Children of Nemed formed a great army to challenge the Fomorians. After a bloody battle their forces were victorious, but could not dislodge Conann the Fomorian king from his enchanted tower of glass. Eventually Conann accepted the challenge of Fergus, son of Nemed, to meet him in single combat.

Fergus prevailed, but in a further battle the Fomorians and the forces of the Children of Nemed were swept to their deaths by a giant wave. Only a handful of Fomorians and 30 of the Children of Nemed survived. The remaining Children of Nemed split into groups and left Ireland, some returning to Greece, and some to central and northern Scotland to become the Picts, and to mainland Britain to become the Britons.

The Coming of the Fir Bolg

After many years, the Greek-settled descendants of the Children of Nemed, known as the Fir Bolg, returned to Ireland and divided the country into five provinces that survive to this day; Ulster, Connacht, Munster, Leinster and Meath. The Fir Bolg introduced the concept of rule by kingship rather than warlord, and Ireland entered into a short period of peaceful prosperity.

Conquest by Gods — the Tuatha Dé Danann

Meanwhile in the 'northern islands of the world', the children of Bethach, grandson of Nemed, gradually began to prosper once again. They were known as the Tuatha Dé Danann, and became skilled in the magic arts and in the arts of the druid-like 'heathen sages'. They were divine in name and status. Their armies fought using both great courage and magic to overcome their enemies. In a later recension of *Lebor Gabála Érenn*, they were forced by the Philistines to flee Greece after they had sided with the Athenians in a war. They travelled west, taking with them their most precious possessions, including the ever-full cauldron of the Dadga, the great father-god of Ireland, and the invincible sword of Núadu.

The Tuatha Dé decided that they must reclaim Ireland, their rightful ancestral home.

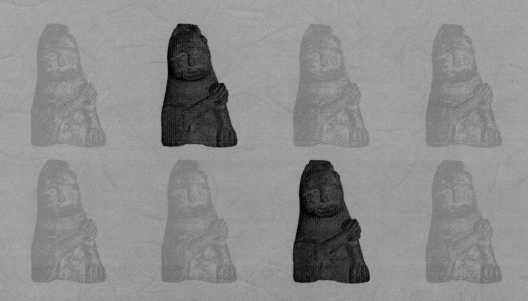

The Hand of Núadu

The Fir Bolg were finally defeated at the first Battle of Moytura. The Tuatha Dé offered their defeated foes the choice of any of the five provinces of Ireland to make their home, and the Fir Bolg chose Connacht. In the battle the hand of Núadu, the leader of the Tuatha Dé, was cut off, and being now imperfect he had to cede his leadership. The Tuatha Dé unwisely chose Bres, son of Elatha, to be their leader, thinking to cement an alliance between the Tuatha Dé and the Fomorians.

The Second Battle of Moytura

Now the wild and fearful Fomorians betrayed the trust of the Tuatha Dé and put them to work for the Fomorian's evil ends. The Tuatha Dé rebelled against this servitude and gathered their forces at the Plain of Pillars, Moytura (or Mag Tuired, in Irish), where the second great Battle of Moytura took place. After fierce and bloody fighting, Lug killed the most fearsome of the Fomorians, the one-eyed Balor of the piercing eye, and routed the Fomorian army for the last time.

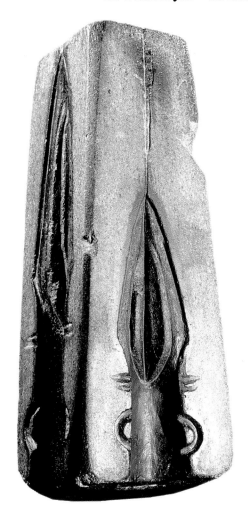

The Last Invasion — the Sons of Mil

The last great invasion of Ireland came at the hands of Donn, Éremón, Éber, Colptha, Amairgen, Ír, Érech Febria, and Érennán, the Sons of Mil. Sailing from their home in Spain with a fleet of 60 ships — 36 for the lords, 24 for their slaves — the Sons of Mil set out to avenge their great-uncle Íth, who had been treacherously put to the sword by the Tuatha Dé. Knowing that the Tuatha Dé were skilled in the magic of the druids, the Sons of Mil brought with them Amairgen, a Son of Mil himself and a poet who had great knowledge of spells and enchantments.

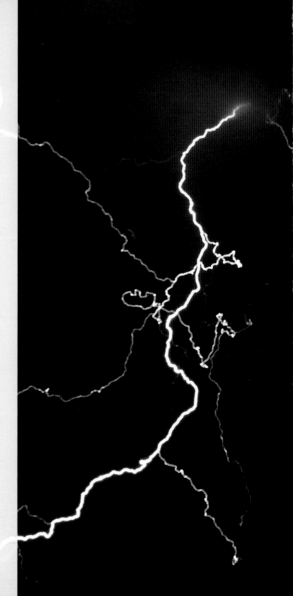

The battles between the Tuatha Dé and the Sons of Míl were mostly supernatural, involving fierce unnatural storms and magically disappearing and reappearing lands. The Sons of Míl eventually overcame the magic of the Tuatha Dé and banished them in a truce that gave them sovereignty of all the territories underground, while the Sons of Míl ruled the land above.

Lines from Lebor Gabála Érenn

Peace high as heaven,

heaven to earth,

earth under heaven

strength in everyone.

Cup's great fullness,

fullness of honey,

mead till satiety

summer in winter.

Spear reliant on shield,

shield reliant on host,

host upon occasion for battle.

The Individual Warrior Hero Prevails — the Ulster Cycle

Set in the provinces of Ulster and Connacht during the reign of King Conchobar mac Nessa, the Ulster Cycle is the most important collection of early Irish myths. In legendary chronology, the events are thought to have taken place from the first century BC, while the texts relating them are no older than the eighth century AD. The Ulster Cycle features the deeds of Cú Chulainn, the foremost of all of Ireland's many great heroes, as he single-handedly defends the province of Ulster from the hostility of neighbouring Connacht.

The major narrative of the Ulster Cycle is the *Táin Bó Cúailnge*, or *Cattle Raid of Cooley*, an epic to rival Virgil or Homer. It is certain moments from this tale on which we shall focus.

How Cú Chulainn Received His Name

As a child, Cú Chulainn was called Sétanta and, from an early age, he showed prodigious strength and courage. One day when he was playing hurling with his friends, his uncle King Conchobar appeared and offered to take him to a feast given by Culann the Smith. Sétanta told the king he would finish his game then follow.

The king and his party carried on their journey and finally arrived at Culann the Smith's house. Culann, thinking all the guests had now arrived, unleashed a giant hound 'which three strong men could not contain' to guard the household, forgetting completely about young Sétanta.

Dispatching the Hound

Sétanta, meanwhile, finished his game, and upon reaching Culann's house was confronted with the snarling hound. Hearing the noise of the dog, the king immediately realized what had happened and was certain his nephew was condemned to die. Undismayed, Sétanta casually dispatched the dog by hurling a *sliotar* ball at him. When Culann realized his prized hound was dead he was desolate, but Sétanta offered to raise a pup to equal the hound. Furthermore, Sétanta said that until the pup was old enough to take the place of the dead dog he himself would be Culann's hound, guarding not only Culann's household, but the whole of the surrounding plain of Muirthemne as well.

From that day forward, the boy Sétanta became known as Cú Chulainn – Culann's Hound.

The Curse of Macha

Macha, a goddess, married Crunnchu mac Agnomain, a wealthy Ulster nobleman. They lived happily together and soon Macha became pregnant. Crunnchu wanted to take part in one of the great seasonal festivals that took place in Ulster, but Macha was afraid he would reveal he had married a goddess, which would spell disaster for them. Although he promised not to, Crunnchu boasted of his wife's speed as a runner, and Macha was forced to race the king's horses. She won, but the exertion caused her to die in childbirth.

As she lay dying, she cursed the men of Ulster so that for nine generations they would be as weak and helpless in battle as a woman in labour.

A Royal Argument

The fearsome Queen Medb (sometimes referred to in the Anglicized form as Maeve), the only woman to command a province, ruled Connacht, Ulster's neighbour, with her consort Ailill mac Máta. Medb was a proud and imperious woman. One night, as she and Ailill lay in bed together, Ailill boasted that he had more riches than his haughty wife. The queen called for all of her possessions and her husband's possessions to be gathered together to see who actually was the richer. It turned out that they were equal in wealth except that Ailill owned a magnificent bull for which Medb had no match.

Queen Medb was furious and asked her adviser Mac Roth were she could find a bull the equal of Ailill's. Mac Roth replied that there was in Ulster a bull as good or better than Ailill's, called the Donn of Cúailnge, owned by Dáire mac Fiachna.

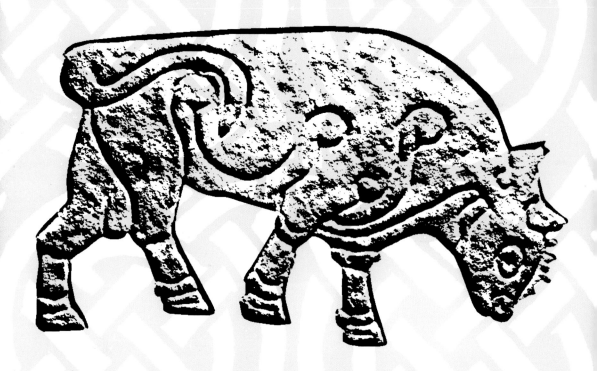

A Failed Negotiation

Queen Medb soon sent Mac Roth to Dáire to ask if he would lend
her his bull for a year to breed with her cows, offering to pay
generously for the loan. Dáire readily agreed and all would have
been well, but at a feast that evening to celebrate, Mac Roth and
his companions became drunk and boastful. They claimed that,
even if Dáire had not agreed, they would still have taken the bull.
Dáire was outraged and swore he would never let
the bull leave Ulster and certainly never set foot in Connacht.

Mac Roth returned home empty-handed
and the stage was set for the cattle raid.

The Raid Begins

Queen Medb was not overly disappointed when Mac Roth returned. She knew of Macha's curse on the men of Ulster and soon gathered a great army from the four remaining provinces of Ireland. As she set out on her quest to steal the Donn of Cúailnge, Fedelm, a prophetess, confronted Medb and, when asked to foretell the outcome of the raid, replied, 'I see nothing but crimson, nothing but red.'

The queen disregarded this ominous prophecy, refusing to believe that her armies were not a match for the cursed men of Ulster. She did not know, however, that Ulster's greatest warrior, Cú Chulainn, was not affected by the curse and vowed to defend Ulster single-handed until Macha's curse was lifted.

Capturing the Bull

Although Queen Medb eventually lost the battle, she initially got what she wanted — the great bull. During the heat of the battle, she sent some of her best warriors behind the Ulster lines. Once free from the battle, they lost no time in getting to Dáire's estate, and quickly captured the Donn of Cúailnge, sending the beast back to Connacht by a little known track.

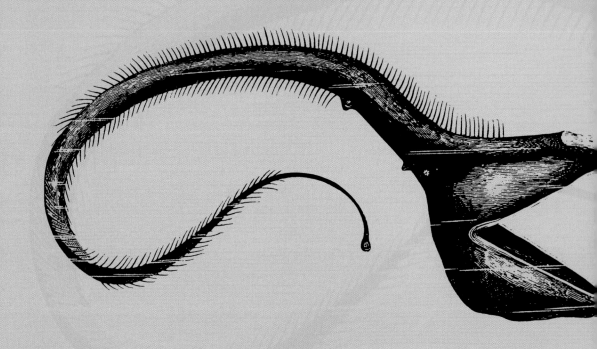

Morrígan the Shape Shifter

For three months, from the feast of Samhain until the feast of Imbolc, Cú Chulainn was good to his word and defeated all the forces that Queen Medb could throw at him. The queen of Connacht was not above being dishonourable in battle and tried everything she could to defeat the young Ulster warrior. She also had help from Morrígan ...

When Cú Chulainn was battling with Lóch mac Emonis in a river, Morrígan, the shape-shifting goddess of war, took on the guise of an enormous black eel and attacked him. Cú Chulainn grasped the monstrous eel and, dashing it against a rock, broke its back. At that moment, Morrígan changed into a snarling she-wolf and finally a hornless red heifer. Cú Chulainn not only wounded Morrígan in all her forms, but also managed to kill Lóch mac Emonis with the *gae bolga*, a magical spear.

Cú Chulainn's Divine Father Intervenes

Exhausted from his efforts in the ongoing battle, Cú Chulainn lay close to death when he saw a handsome young warrior approaching in the distance. The figure appeared wearing a green cloak fastened by a fabulous silver brooch and carrying a five-pointed spear, a javelin and a black shield. Cú Chulainn realized that this was surely someone from the Otherworld. Indeed, the warrior announced that he was Lug of the Long Arm, Cú Chulainn's true father.

Follamain's Young Army

Lug told Cú Chulainn to sleep while he, Lug, continued the fight in Cú Chulainn's place. While Cú Chulainn recovered his strength, an army of young Ulstermen, led by Conchobar's son Follamain and unaffected by Macha's curse on their elders, joined the fray. They fought with the armies of Connacht three times, killing more than three times their number. Eventually they were overcome by sheer force of numbers, and every one of the young Ulster army was killed, including the king's son.

Cú Chulainn Returns to Fight on the Plain of Muirthemne

For three days and three nights, Cú Chulainn lay in a healing coma. On the morning of the fourth day, he rose from his sleep to discover the terrible fate of his young countrymen. Now he transcended his human nature and became superhuman in the wreaking of his vengeance for the death of so many of his fellow Ulster youths. According to the *Brislech Mór Maige Muirthemne* (The Great Destruction of the Plain of Muirthemne), Chulainn felled one foe after another on a great rampage in his war chariot.

Brother against Brother

Medb eventually managed to send Cú Chulainn's foster brother, Fer Diad, to fight him. Fer Diad was cajoled with threats of satire and dishonour, promised various prizes for fighting Cú Chulainn and in the end was convinced by Medb's lie that Cú Chulainn had boasted he could beat Fer Diad. For four days Fer Diad and Cú Chulainn fought until, in desperation, Cú Chulainn called for the *gae bolga*, with which he finally killed his foster brother.

Cú Chulainn Finishes off His Enemies

Finally, Cú Chulainn encountered his foster father, the exiled Fergus mac Roich, whom he forced to retreat before him in recompense for an earlier retreat of Cú Chulainn's from Fergus in battle. Once Fergus had left the field of battle, taking with him his band of Ulster exiles, Queen Medb and Ailill were left to face Cú Chulainn with only the remnants of the Connacht army. Cú Chulainn finally destroyed the last of his enemies, but in a moment of magnanimity allowed Medb and Ailill and their few remaining warriors safe passage back to Connacht.

Cú Chulainn Speaks of His Deeds

Skilful my warrior exploits.

Fearful blows I strike

against a ghostly army.

I take battle to many hosts,

death-dealing destruction

to the brave troops of Medb and Ailill.

A cold-blooded treachery

perpetrated by a woman's mind

requires good counsel, wisely taken,

to combat courageous men

and overcome them

by heroic exploits.

The Two Bulls Clash

When the Donn arrived in Connacht, Aillil's bull, Findbennach, heard the Donn's bellowed cries of defiance. There was room for only one great bull in Connacht, and a bloody fight ensued. The two mighty beasts fought for a day and a night, circling the whole of Ireland in their frenzy to emerge the victor. The Donn of Cúailnge finally overcame the white-horned Findbennach, and returned to his homeland at Cooley — but not before first ranging over the midlands, and flinging parts of the Findbennach across Ireland; hence the name Cruachan (now Rathcroghan), so-called because he left there a heap (*crúach*) of the Findbennach's liver. On his return to Cooley, he trampled the youths and women who were lamenting him there, and then — according to some — he simply collapsed and died. And such was the fate of the Donn of Cúailnge.

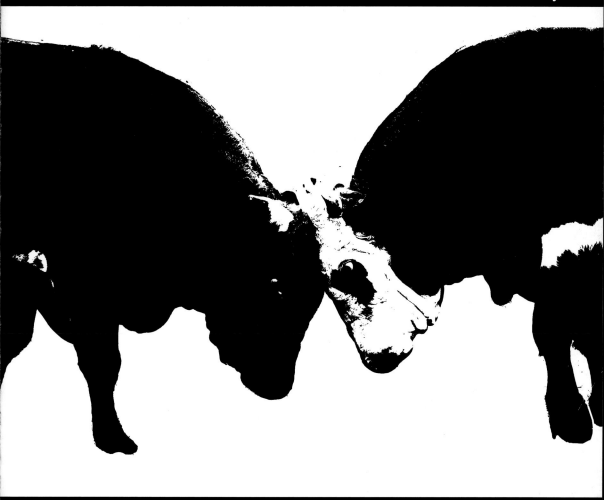

Comradeship, Noble Conduct and Otherworldly Adventures — the Fenian Cycle

The Fenian Cycle is the third of the great Irish story cycles and is set in the third century AD. The earliest Fianna texts date from the eighth century. They tell the story of the Fianna, a band of travelling warriors owing allegiance to their leader rather than to a province or clan.

Although there are many great warriors featured in the Fenian Cycle, the greatest of them is Finn mac Cumhaill — Fionn in the Modern Irish spelling and Finn McCool in the Anglicized version — a Leinster chieftain (although he is also from Munster or Ulster, depending on the source text). Finn is surely one of the greatest names of any hero in history.

A Bloody Feud

The Fenian Cycle takes place against the backdrop of the bloody and unrelenting feud between the clans of Baíscne and Morna, who were in conflict for the supremacy of the Fianna of Ireland. At the start of the cycle, Cumhaill of the Clan Baíscne is killed and beheaded by Goll, the one-eyed leader of the Clan Morna, who makes off with Cumhaill's head and all his possessions. Cumhaill's widow is pregnant and gives birth to a boy, Deimne, who she hides in the forests of Slieve Bloom, fearing further violence from the Morna clan.

She leaves the boy in the care of Fiacail, a warrior, and two powerful women — Bodbmall, Fiacail's wife and a druid priestess, and her sister Liath Luachra (the Grey One of Luachair) — who raise Deimne. He grows up to be both fair and strong, and leaves the forest to avenge his father's death and reclaim his rightful inheritance. Early in his travels, Deimne is given the name Finn (the 'fair one').

The Salmon of knowledge

Hunted by the Morna clan, Finn travelled throughout Ireland serving many of the kings and high lords of the country, becoming a feared and respected warrior. Like many Celtic heroes, however, he also became well versed in magic and poetry, spending time with Finnéces, an aged poet and seer. The poet lived on the banks of the River Boyne, where for seven long years he sought the Salmon of Knowledge, a fish that would give whoever ate it the power to foretell the future and understand the past.

During Finn's stay, Finnéces finally caught the salmon and gave it to Finn to cook for him, telling him to eat none of it. Finn burnt his fingers on the hot fish and put them into his mouth to cool them down, and the poet, realizing that the salmon was destined for Finn, let him eat it. By eating the salmon, Finn gained the knowledge of all things and the wisdom to understand them.

An Enchanted Pool

Milucra the fairy daughter of Culann the Smith (a different smith to the Culann of Cú Chulainn's naming tale) vied for Finn's heart with her sister, Áine, who had vowed only to marry a man who had flowing golden hair like Finn.

One day Milucra tricked Finn into diving into an enchanted pool while hunting on the slopes of Slieve Gullion. When Finn emerged from the pool, he became old and wizened, and his hair turned silver grey. His warriors realized what had happened and sought out Milucra to force her to change Finn back to his younger self. This she did, but to outwit her sister she refused to change his hair back to its original colour and it remained silver grey. Her efforts were in vain, for Finn never returned to Slieve Gullion.

A Magical Transformation

On another day's hunting, Finn met the woman who was to be his favourite wife. This is how it happened. Finn spotted a young doe and gave chase with his fellow hunters. The doe was so fleet of foot that it outran everyone but Finn and his two hounds. When the hounds finally caught the creature, instead of falling on it and killing it, they were playing happily with it when Finn found them.

Finn knew that this was no normal doe and took it back to his camp. That night a beautiful woman appeared. She told Finn that she was Sadb, a noblewoman who had been turned into a doe by an evil druid whose advances she had rejected. Because he spared her in the hunt, Finn had broken the druid's enchantment. The two fell deeply in love, and Sadb bore a child, Oisín, who was destined to become another great Irish hero.

A Tragic Childhood

When it was almost time for Sadb to give birth, Finn was compelled to leave her to fight an army of raiders from the kingdom of Lochlann on the west coast of Scotland. While he was away, Fer Doirich, the dark druid who had first turned Sadb into a doe, returned disguised as Finn and once again transformed Sadb.

Finn was distraught and searched the whole of Ireland for his love, but to no avail. Eventually, while out hunting, his hounds came across a wild child, naked and covered entirely with hair. When Finn caught up with his hounds, they were playing with the boy as they had with the doe. Finn soon realized that the boy must be his son, and called the boy Oisín, which means 'little fawn', but they never saw his mother Sadb again.

The Fianna

To even be considered for membership of the
Fianna a young warrior must first prove he could:

- run like the wind across all kinds of terrain

- be master both of sword and axe

- hunt fearlessly all day on horseback and foot

- jump a bar placed at least as high as his forehead

- track silently through the forest for hour after
  hour, disturbing neither leaf nor twig

- write and recite poetry of the highest standard

The Mysterious Lords of Irúaith

Many warriors came to Finn's court to join the Fianna, but none was more mysterious than the three Lords of Irúaith, who arrived accompanied by a huge female hound whose coat contained every colour known to man. Every night, the brothers withdrew from the court to a small camp of their own.

A wall of fire surrounded the Lords of Irúaith's camp, and they demanded that under no circumstances should anyone spy on them. They explained that they were under a terrible spell. Each night one of them died and the other two had to keep vigil over him. Providing they kept watch all night, the one who died would be restored to life. Nothing must interfere with their vigil or a brother would die.

The Lords of Irúaith Prove Their Worth

Three more strangers appeared at Finn's court. They said they were Harm, Plunder and Famine, the sons of Uar. They had come to demand a blood price for the death of their father, slain in battle by one of the Fianna. Finn refused their demand, as Uar had been fairly slain in combat. The brothers vowed to extract a terrible revenge and went about laying waste to Finn's land.

The Fianna were powerless against the might of the sons of Uar, so the Lords of Irúaith offered to intervene. They enchanted Harm, Plunder and Famine ,making them too weak to fight, then set their giant hound on them. The hound chased the sons of Uar off a high cliff and, they fell to their deaths in the foaming sea below.

The Lords of Irúaith Leave in Anger

The desire to know exactly what went on in the Lords of Irúaith's camp proved too much for two of Finn's warriors. One night they crept up to the Lords' camp, and this is what they saw:

Two of the lords sat in front of the third lord, who was lying on the ground with their hound – which was now no more than the size of a lapdog – sitting on his chest. The hound spewed forth choice liquors on demand for the three lords. The two Fianna warriors watched in dumbstruck amazement until the Lords of Irúaith soon became aware of their presence, whereupon the hound emitted a magical wind from beneath her tail, depriving the men of their armour and weapons, causing them to die in the wall of flames. She then made ashes of their bodies with her magical breath.

An Ominous Prediction

After the untimely death of his wife Sadb, Finn spent the rest of his life leading the warriors of the Fianna, fighting against evil the length and breadth of Ireland. There was no warrior who could match Finn's valour and wisdom, and he was respected and honoured throughout the land. In Finn's youth, it had been prophesied that he would die in Ireland in a certain year. That year was now approaching, and Finn resolved to leave his beloved country and spend the year in Scotland, thus avoiding the prophecy.

The warriors of the Fianna were dismayed when they heard the news and vowed to protect him, by taking it in turn to receive him as their guest in their strongholds. The warriors' love for their great leader touched Finn, and he decided to remain in Ireland, trusting his faithful Fianna to protect him from any threat of evil.

A Grandson's Revenge

Finn gathered together some 150 of his bravest warriors and began his journey from stronghold to stronghold. His first host was Fer Tai, husband of the daughter of Goll mac Morna. Fer Tai was a faithful member of the Fianna, but his son Fer Lí had never forgiven Finn for the killing of his grandfather.

At the welcoming banquet, Fer Lí unjustly accused Finn's men of stealing their cattle. A great fight ensued, and it took Fer Lí's mother to bring the fighting to an end, berating her son for mistreating their guests under their roof. Fer Lí obeyed his mother, but challenged Finn's men to do battle the next day at Áth Brea, a ford on the River Boyne.

The Battle at Áth Brea

When Finn's 150 warriors arrived at the field of battle, they found a force of more than 3,000 ranged against them. Finn immediately realized that defeat was inevitable and sued for peace, but Fer Lí twice rejected his terms. Wearily Finn prepared to do battle for the last time.

As the war trumpets blared, the Fenian warriors bravely attacked the great army of Fer Lí, knowing their cause was lost. The warriors battled heroically to the last man, steadfastly refusing to concede victory to the overwhelmingly larger horde. Finally every one of the Fenians was slain, and Finn, greatest of all Ireland's great warriors, fell in the heat of battle fighting alongside his men.

The Gods Intervene

A great warrior such as Finn mac Cumhaill could not be allowed to die such an ignominious death, so unfairly outnumbered by a violent bloodthirsty horde. So, it is sometimes said that the gods of the Otherworld secretly spirited away the bodies of Finn and his brave Fenian warriors to the Sídhe, their underground world. Here in the Otherworld, Finn and his warriors slept – not dead but merely resting, ready to come to the aid of Ireland again should the country ever be in danger.

Voyages and Adventures

There are many stories of voyages and adventures that together form an important part of Celtic mythology. The voyages (*immrama* in Irish mythology) are concerned mainly with the journey, whereas the adventures (*echtrae* in Irish mythology) often describe what happens when the travellers reach their destination, usually in the Otherworld.

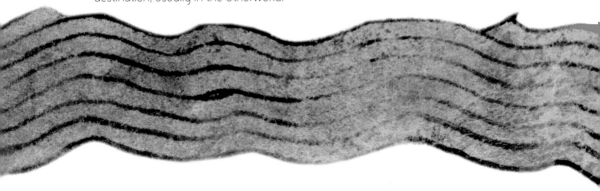

Connla the Red Is Bewitched

Connla, son of Conn of the Hundred Battles, spent much of his days travelling the kingdom, watching, lest the gods of the Otherworld rise up to reclaim the land above ground that they had ceded to the Sons of Mil so many years ago.

One day a beautiful young woman approached Connla and announced that she came from Mag Mell, a land in the Otherworld where there was no sickness or death. In this enchanted place, the days were spent feasting and the nights carousing and lovemaking. Although his father advised him against it, Connla was unable to resist the lure of the maiden and her tales of the Otherworld. Finally, when Conn could do no more to dissuade his son, Connla and the maiden sailed away in a crystal coracle, never to be seen or heard of again.

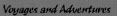

King Cormac Receives a Silver Branch

One day a stern grey-haired warrior visited Cormac in his great court at Tara. The warrior told the king that he came from a place called the Land of Promise where nothing decayed or grew old, where no one was ever sorrowful or melancholy, and where pride and envy were unknown.

Cormac was impressed with the stranger and suggested a pact of friendship. To seal the pact, the warrior offered Cormac a silver branch on which were three golden apples. In exchange for the branch, which made the most wonderful soothing music, Cormac agreed to grant the stranger three requests. The stranger left vowing to return.

Three Terrible Requests

The stranger did indeed return to the court at Tara. Three times he came and each time his request was more awful than the last. The first time he asked for Cormac's daughter Ailbe, the second time he demanded Cairbre, Cormac's son, and finally he asked for Eithne, the queen of Tara and Cormac's wife. This last request was too much for Cormac and, although he agreed, he followed the stranger with a group of his bravest warriors. As they pursued the stranger, they were enveloped in a magic mist conjured up by the grey-haired warrior, and the king found himself alone, separated from his men. Cormac passed through a wondrous land in which strange scenes unfolded before him, before reaching a fortress with silver ramparts. Cormac knew he must be in the Otherworld and entered the great hall of the fortress to learn his fate.

The Golden Cup of Truth

As the inhabitants of the Otherworld prepared their evening meal, they each told stories. If the stories they told were untrue, the food would not cook. Cormac told his story of how he had lost his son, his daughter and his wife, and had set out with his warriors to find them. As he told his story he wept, and the people of the Otherworld were much affected by his grief.

The grey-haired stranger reappeared as a handsome young warrior and gave Cormac a beautiful cup. The cup was exquisitely fashioned from the purest gold, and the warrior (who was Manannán mac Lir) told Cormac that he could use it to tell truth from falsehood. As Cormac had been good to his word and allowed even the greatest of the warrior's requests, the bond between the Otherworld and Cormac's kingdom was confirmed. Cormac slept and, when he awoke, he found himself in his court at Tara, surrounded by his family.

The Voyage of the Son of Ailill Ochair Ága

Máel Dúin was the son of Ailill Ochair Ága, a brave warrior cut down in his youth by treacherous villains. His mother was a nun who, wishing to keep the circumstances of his birth a secret, entreated the queen of a nearby kingdom to raise the boy as if he was her own. The tale of Máel Dúin is in essence a penitential Christian one.

As the boy Máel Dúin grew to manhood, he became skilled not only in the ways of war, but also in the more gentle arts of poetry and music. However, he never felt quite at ease with his foster brothers who were, truth be told, jealous of his many courtly attributes. Eventually he could stand the teasing of his foster brothers no longer and begged the queen to tell him of his origins.

Máel Dúin Learns the Secret of His Birth

Against her will, the queen eventually succumbed to Máel Dúin's pleading and told him the tragic tale of his father's death and of her promise to his mother. At once Máel Dúin swore to avenge the death of his father no matter what it might take or wherever he must travel. With the help of a Druid, he built an enchanted coracle with three hulls. The boat was able to hold a small band of warriors and, having chosen the finest young fighters he could muster, Máel Dúin set off on his quest to find and slay his father's killers.

Máel Dúin and his men were to endure a long and arduous journey, encountering many different islands on the way. The first island they discovered was, in fact, where the slayers of his father were located, but before they could act they were blown away by an adverse wind.

Ants, Birds and Beasts

After drifting for three days and three nights, Máel Dúin and his men came upon an island swarming with ants each the size of a foal. The creatures seemed bloodthirsty and so the men sailed on, next coming to an island populated by many birds and surrounded by trees. Máel Dúin bravely went ashore and found that there was no danger. The crew was able to eat its fill of birds and stock up its food stores with even more of them. On the next island, the voyageurs beheld a fearsome horse-like beast with sharp claws, and on the next an equally frightening scene of giant horses and riders racing against each other as fast as the wind and to the deafening roar of the crowd.

303

Much-needed Nourishment

As the travellers sailed the seas, they became hungrier and hungrier, and thirstier and thirstier. When they reached an island with a house the door of which was letting through hordes of salmon thrown from the sea, they entered and feasted on the food that they found laid out by the residents' beds. When they came upon a wooded island surrounded by cliffs, Máel Dúin reached over and broke off a branch, which after three days and three nights grew three apples that each time sustained the crew for 40 nights.

More Beasts

Máel Dúin and his men were to meet yet more monstrous creatures, including, on the next island, a great beast who roamed around and whose body revolved inside its skin and whose skin revolved around its body. After escaping the rain of stones thrown at them by this monster, the travellers in their boat came upon the next island, where horse-like creatures tore chunks out of each other's sides and the land ran with blood. Leaving that island quickly, they then reached an island with more beasts – this time firey red swine-like creatures. When these beasts retired into caverns under the ground, the men were able to take apples from the trees that grew there and replenish their supplies.

The Deserted Palace

After almost three weeks at sea, and after coming upon nine other islands, with their food and water almost gone they came upon an uninhabited island on which stood a white palace. They entered the deserted palace only to find a huge treasure hoard piled high on the floor of the main hall. The only living thing in the whole palace was a little cat that seemed quite uninterested in the young warriors.

As they wondered at the fabulous treasure that lay at their feet, the warriors noticed a great table laden with food and drink. Hungry and thirsty from their long voyage, Máel Dúin's men fell upon the feast and ate their fill. After they had eaten, they slept and upon waking gathered up the remaining food to take back to their ship. Some of the warriors wanted to take the treasure as well, but Máel Dúin forbade it.

The Little Cat Strikes

One of the youngest warriors was unable to resist the lure of the gold and jewellery, and as he left the palace he put a golden torque into a pocket in his tunic. Thinking no one had noticed, the young warrior walked out of the palace followed by the little white cat. No sooner was he out of the palace grounds than the cat leapt up at him like a blazing fiery arrow and he was magically consumed in fire. The warrior fell to the ground and disappeared leaving nothing more than a small pile of smouldering ash. The cat casually returned to the palace. Máel Dúin picked up the torque and returned it to the great hall. This pleased the little cat, which now sat purring quietly. With heavy hearts, the warriors returned to their boat.

Mysterious Islands

As Máel Dúin and his band of warriors sailed the seas in search of Aillil's killers they were to come across many more strange islands. On one they saw a man who seemed to do little all day but change sheep from black to white and back again; on another they were almost ensnared, as all who landed there were overcome by a great sadness and were unable to leave. Although they discovered these many lands, they could not return to the place that harboured the villains who had cut down their leader's father. One day they heard in the distance what sounded like hundreds of people all talking at once. As they rowed towards the babble of voices, a huge rock appeared out of the sea covered in birds. Search as the warriors would, they could see no sign of humans on the outcrop and could only assume that the noises they heard were made by the birds.

The Hermit's Secret

The warriors could make no sense of the voices they heard and, as they wondered at this strange apparition, one of them noticed another island not far away. Leaving the babbling birds, they made for this second island, where they found many more birds. These birds were silent, however, and, unlike the first island, this one had a human inhabitant in the form of an ancient recluse.

Máel Dúin and his crew quickly landed and questioned the old man. He was a Christian and told of his pilgrimage and how his coracle had been made unsteady. He had placed sods of earth in it to steady it, then God had turned these gradually into the island for him. The birds on the island were the souls of his family that had passed away and who remained on the island waiting for the Day of Judgement.

The Island of the Women

After yet more weird and wonderful experiences, including encountering a miraculous fountain and an underwater island, Máel Dúin and his men arrived at an island that was home to 17 maidens. They were warmly welcomed, bathed and fed by the women, and for three months of winter lived and slept with the maidens in paradise. When they then tried to leave on their boat, however, the queen flung a thread which stuck to Máel Dúin's hand and with this she drew them back to shore. So they stayed three more months. Finally they escaped when one of the men let the thread stick to his hand instead, then cut off his hand, thereby releasing it and the thread into the sea and enabling the crew to sail away.

Máel Dúin Is Made an Offer

The last person that Máel Dúin met on his long voyage was another hermit, dressed only in his white hair, who told them a long story of penitence for his previous haughty ways. Máel Dúin listened intently to the old man and quickly realized that he was extremely wise. The hermit prepared the hungry warriors a hearty meal, and during the feast Máel Dúin asked the old man if he knew where the men who had slain his father could be found. The hermit replied that he could indeed tell them where to find the villains, but only on the condition that Máel Dúin swore neither to kill or to harm the men when he found them. He should spare them in thanks for his escape from the many dangers he had encountered on his journey, and for his safe return to his homeland.

Máel Dúin Makes a Wise Decision

Máel Dúin reflected for a while and saw the wisdom of the old man's words, hard though they were. He realized that God had been protecting his men throughout their arduous journey and that if God wished the villains' lives to be spared he must obey.

So it was that Máel Dúin, after a voyage full of incredible adventures and amazing encounters, eventually found the men who had killed his father, but rather than take his revenge he made peace with them.

Wooings, Betrothals and Tragic Romances

A recurring theme throughout Celtic mythology is the power of love and how it can bring not only great happiness, but also very real tragedy. In the myths we have recounted so far, we have seen great heroes born of the marriage of humans and the denizens of the Otherworld, princes lured away by the promise of eternal happiness, and lovers parted by violent death.

One of the most famous of the romantic myths of Celtic origin is the tale of Tristan and Iseult (which is of both Irish and Welsh or Brittonic origin, although incidentally all of the versions of the tale which are complete and well known are either French or German). It is a story that echoes down through the ages and has resonances in the mythologies of other great civilizations. But there were many other great romantic tales, too.

The Love Triangle of Finn, Diarmuid and Gráinne

When the great Irish hero Finn mac Cumhaill was growing old, the Fianna thought he should have a new wife to comfort him in his later years, and Finn agreed. He chose Gráinne, the beautiful young daughter of the king Cormac mac Airt. Cormac happily consented to the match, and Finn set off for Tara, the sacred and noble seat of the kings of Ireland, to claim his new wife. Most handsome of his noble party was Diarmuid, the same warrior who had been given the love spot by a fair maiden from the Otherworld.

When Finn arrived at Tara, Gráinne was dismayed to find that she was betrothed to such an old man, albeit one of Ireland's greatest heroes. Her heart was set on handsome Diarmuid, and she would countenance no other.

Gráinne's Scheming

Diarmuid was a noble and honest warrior, and one of the greatest of the Fianna. When Gráinne professed her love to him he protested, saying that he would never think of wooing any woman who was promised to his lord.

Gráinne ignored Diarmuid's noble words and put a *geis* (a ritual injunction) on him so he was unable to resist her advances. He turned to his comrade Oisín, Finn's son, for advice. Oisín knew that, because of the *geis* that Gráinne had placed on him, Diarmuid had no choice but to flee with Gráinne that very night.

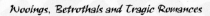

The Couple Incurs Finn's Wrath

While Finn and Cormac slept, drugged by Gráinne, Diarmuid and his newfound love fled into the night. When Finn awoke from his unnatural slumber, he was furious to hear that his bride-to-be had left with one of his most valued warriors. He swore undying enmity towards Diarmuid and spent all of his energy tracking down the fleeing lovers, pursuing them when he could, and sending the Fianna to track them down and kill them for their treachery. There followed various adventures, one of which had Diarmuid defeating the one-eyed giant Searbhan with the giant's own club, after Finn had demanded his men to fetch berries from the tree guarded by Searbhan or bring him Diarmuid's head.

After several months, the bewitched warrior finally fell in love with his beautiful bride and she bore him four fine sons and one daughter. Eventually, Oengus, the foster father and protector of Diarmuid, took advantage of Finn's weariness of the pursuit and persuaded him to make peace with Diarmuid.

An Old Wound that Never Healed

Although it seemed that all was well between the two great warriors, Finn had never truly forgiven Diarmuid for spiriting away the fair Gráinne – though it must be said that Diarmuid was really the innocent victim of Gráinne's wiles.

Finn could not forget Diarmuid's slight to his honour, innocent or not. By tricking Diarmuid into fighting a boar, Finn made Diarmuid break a *geis* that had been placed on him forbidding him to kill any boar, for the boar was enchanted to have the same length of life as Diarmuid, and the boar was destined therefore to kill Diarmuid.

A Great Warrior Shamed

As Diarmuid lay dying, he begged Finn to save him, for he knew that Finn had the power to heal his wounds. But the once-noble Finn could not find it in his heart to save his comrade of old, such was the bitterness he felt for the loss of Gráinne. Three times Diarmuid pleaded for his life, and three times Finn denied him.

Even the most loyal of the Fianna could see that Finn's behaviour was not befitting a noble hero, and they begged him to save Diarmuid. Finn was unmoved by their words and watched his old comrade slowly die. At the very last Finn relented, but he was too late to save Diarmuid, who passed away with the laments of the Fianna ringing in his ears. Thus was a great warrior lost and another disgraced by the power of love for a woman.

Tristan and Iseult

The story of Tristan and his love for Iseult has a complex history that is shrouded in the mists of Irish and Welsh mythology. Although we associate the tale with the Arthurian legends, it is probable that the original story pre-dates the court of King Arthur and has echoes in the story of Gráinne's love for Diarmuid, among other tales. The story usually has Tristan and Iseult inadvertently consuming a love potion that seals their love for each other and leads them to carry on a long affair despite Iseult marrying King Mark of Cornwall. Iseult ultimately remains with Mark, while Tristan lives and dies in exile. As we shall see, in the quite different and very late Welsh version that follows, Iseult's wisdom and cunning fashion a far happier ending.

Tristan Falls in Love with the Wife of His King

It happened that Tristan, a nobleman and brave warrior, fell hopelessly in love with Iseult, the wife of his king and uncle, Mark ap Meirchion. Enraged by the insult he had suffered, King Mark insisted that King Arthur should avenge the deed. Arthur agreed to go to the forest with his knights and seek from Tristan 'either satisfaction or bloodshed'.

When Iseult heard of this, she feared for her lover's safety, but Tristan, speaking in the poetic verse form known as *englyn*, reassured his love.

Tristan's Englyn

Fair Iseult be not afraid;

for while I protect thee

three hundred knights

will not succeed in carrying thee off,

nor three hundred armed men

Arthur Intervenes

Not wanting to kill Tristan, King Arthur persuaded him to leave the woods and meet with him so that they could resolve the matter (and some tales even have Sir Gawain doing so on Arthur's behalf). Tristan agreed to talk with King Arthur and abide by whatever decision Arthur made. Arthur brought the two warring suitors together, but neither Tristan nor King Mark would agree to give up the hand of fair Iseult to the other.

Arthur's Solution and King Mark's Decision

King Arthur realized that neither party would willingly back down, so he proposed this solution. One should have Iseult while the leaves were on the trees, and the other would have her when the trees had no leaves. Furthermore, King Mark, as the lawful husband of Iseult, could make the choice, which Tristan must abide by.

King Mark decided to have the hand of Iseult while there were no leaves on the trees because, 'when the trees have not leaves, the nights are longest'.

Iseult's Response

When she heard Arthur's judgement and King Mark's decision Iseult rejoiced, praising Arthur for his great wisdom, and she sang the following *englyn:*

> Three trees are good in nature:
> the holly, the ivy and the yew,
> which keep their leaves throughout their lives:
> I am Tristan's for as long as he may live.

So King Mark lost his wife to Tristan for ever, and thus ends this version of the story of Tristan and Iseult.

The Mabinogi — the Great Welsh Story Cycle

The majority of the Celtic myths that have survived are from Ireland, but there is one great story cycle from Wales, the *Mabinogi*. The *Mabinogi* stories appear in The White Book of Rhydderch and The Red Book of Hergst, manuscripts which date to the early fourteenth century (although it has been argued that the cycle existed as early as the eleventh to twelfth centuries). The *Mabinogi* is made up of the Four Branches, translated as follows: *Pwyll Prince of Dyfed*, *Branwen daughter of Llyr*, *Manawydan son of Llyr*, and *Math son of Mathonwy*. The stories were not translated into English in their entirety until the middle of the nineteenth century, when Lady Charlotte Guest translated the *Mabinogi*, along with several other medieval Welsh prose works, in three volumes, *The Four Branches of the Mabinogi*, *The Four Independent Native Tales* and the *Three Romances*.

A Superhuman Horsewoman

The First Branch of the *Mabinogi* details the quest of Pwyll, Lord of Dyfed, to win the hand of Rhiannon, an Otherworldly woman. Pwyll first encountered Rhiannon at the sacred Mound of Arberth, where she appeared riding a pure white stallion. Pwyll was immediately smitten by her beauty and asked one of his men to approach her and discover her name, but she rode off, and no matter how fast Pwyll's man rode he could not overtake her. The second day went much as the first, with Pwyll's man unable to catch up to the mysterious lady.

On the third day, Pwyll returned to the spot mounted on his fastest steed, but try as he might he could not outrun the fair maiden and her snow-white horse. Eventually he was forced to call out to her, begging her to stop in the name of love.

GORDON WAIN 1984

RHIANNON
DAUGHTER OF
NEFEYDD

Rhiannon Tells Her Story

Rhiannon pulled up her horse, telling Pwyll she would gladly have stopped sooner had he asked, for it was Pwyll that she had come to speak with. The fair maiden explained to Pwyll that she had been promised to a man against her will and had refused to give her hand to him. She continued that she had seen Pwyll from afar and had fallen in love with him, rejecting all other offers of marriage in the hope that he would accept her.

Pwyll was overjoyed to hear this and enquired of Rhiannon what he must do. She told him to come to her father King Hefeydd's palace in a year's time, when she would prepare a feast for him where he could ask her father for her hand in marriage.

Pwyll Makes a Terrible Mistake

Pwyll arrived at the king's court with a hundred of his bravest men, and they were received with great honour. As Pwyll was enjoying the feast, a stranger entered the great hall, saying that he had come to ask a favour of Pwyll. Pwyll graciously replied that he would do whatever was in his power to grant the stranger's request, little realizing that the stranger was Gwawl, the nobleman to whom Rhiannon was betrothed against her wish. Gwawl demanded of Pwyll the hand of Rhiannon and furthermore that a wedding feast should be prepared to celebrate the match. Pwyll now realized his awful mistake, but his code of honour bound him to keep his pledge. Rhiannon upbraided Pwyll for his rashness, but said she might still find a way for them to be together. She told Gwawl that this feast was for Pwyll, but if Gwawl returned a year later she would prepare a feast for him.

A Second Wedding Feast

The 12 months passed, and Gwawl returned to Hefeydd's court to claim his bride. Rhiannon had prepared a feast as she agreed, but during the year she had been in contact with Pwyll and had told him of her plan to trick Gwawl. So it was that, while Gwawl and his men were feasting in the great hall, Pwyll and his men were waiting in a nearby orchard dressed in threadbare clothing and worn-out boots.

As soon as the first course was over, Pwyll entered the feast carrying an enchanted sack that Rhiannon had made for him. Disguised as a peasant, Pwyll was not recognized by Gwawl, who asked him what his business was. Pwyll asked for a favour, but Gwawl was more cautious in his answer than Pwyll had been, agreeing to any request that Gwawl considered was reasonable.

Gwawl Grants a Favour

Pwyll produced the sack and asked Gwawl if he could fill the bag with food from the remnants of the feast. Gwawl willingly agreed, but his men found that no matter how much food they put in the sack it was never even half full. Despairing of ever filling the sack, Gwawl cried out to know how it should be done. Pwyll replied that when a noble man of wealth and status stood on the sack and declared that it was full enough that would suffice.

Wishing to be rid of the peasant and his troublesome request, Gwawl got up from the table and stood on the sack, at which moment Pwyll pulled up the sides of the sack, tying them together and trapping Gwawl inside. Once Gwawl was securely imprisoned in the sack, Pwyll's warriors burst in, quickly overpowering Gwawl's men, and kicking the trapped Gwawl in the sack into submission.

357

Pwyll Turns the Tables

Gwawl realized that he had been tricked and that his position was hopeless. He begged for mercy, and Pwyll granted his request on the condition that he never attempt to avenge the deed. Gwawl agreed to the terms and left the king's palace.

So the wedding feast that was to have been Gwawl's became Pwyll's, and the next day he and Rhiannon set off for Pwyll's castle at Arberth to begin their life together. But life was not always happy for the couple, as the rest of the story tells.

A Happy Birth Turns into a Tragic Loss

After some three years of married life, Rhiannon bore Pwyll a long-sought-for son. On the night of his birth, however, the child disappeared. Rhiannon's women in waiting had fallen asleep in the night and were terrified that they would be blamed for the loss of the child and burned at the stake for their negligence. To escape the blame, they smeared Rhiannon's face and hands with blood and accused her of devouring her child before their very eyes. Rhiannon would not defend herself from the women's outrageous accusations, saying that she would rather accept her punishment than even countenance talking to them.

For seven years she sat at the gates of Arberth and had to tell her tragic story to any stranger who passed, offering them rides on her back as if she were a horse.

Lord Teyrnon Makes a Mysterious Discovery

A short while later, one of Lord Pwyll's distant neighbours, Lord Teyrnon of Gwent Ys Coed, discovered a baby wrapped in silken swaddling clothes at the door of his stables. Teyrnon had set a trap for the thief of his foals, but the creature responsible had escaped, apparently leaving behind the child. Not having any idea who the parents might be, he raised the child as his own. The baby grew to be fair, handsome, strong and courageous. At around this time, Lord Teyrnon heard the tragic tale of Lord Pwyll and Rhiannon's child. Due to the child's resemblance to Lord Pwyll, Teyrnon eventually realized that the boy must indeed be Pwyll's long-lost son.

A Happy Reunion

Lord Teyrnon and his wife were sad to lose their adopted son, but they knew that they must return him to his natural parents and free Rhiannon from her terrible and undeserved punishment.

They returned the boy to Pwyll's court and explained the whole story of how they had found and raised the child. Lord Pwyll was overjoyed that the boy, his heir, had been found and that his beloved wife, Rhiannon, could return to his side. The boy grew up to be a valiant and well-liked warrior. He was named Pryderi.

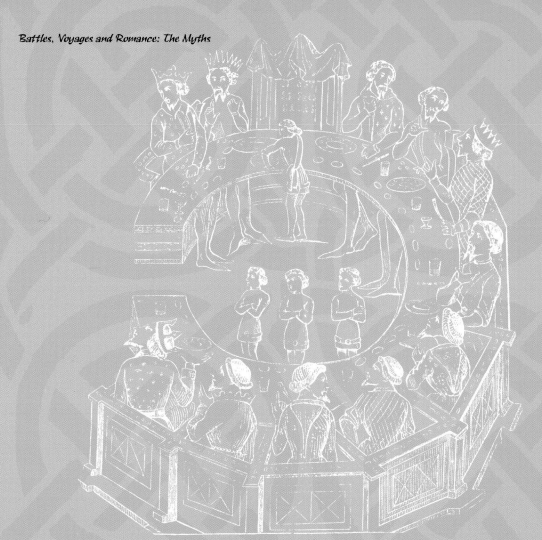

The Great Court of Camelot

The origins of King Arthur are hidden in the dark folds of history. Although the most famous of all Celtic heroes, we do not even know for sure whether Arthur actually existed or whether he was, as some historians suggest, a fictional figure formed from a combination of Celtic deities, an ancient Welsh warrior and a idealized version of a great chieftain.

Whatever Arthur's origins, what we know of him today is largely due to the work of three men, the twelfth-century English historian Geoffrey of Monmouth, the twelfth-century French poet Chrétien de Troyes and the fifteenth-century writer Sir Thomas Malory. To tell the legend of Arthur would take a volume in itself, but let us finish off with one of the best-known stories, from Malory's *Le Morte Darthur* (as spelt in its first printing).

An Unknown Heir to the English Throne

It happened that Uther Pendragon, king of all England, fell hopelessly in love with Igraine, the wife of his rebellious subject the Duke of Tintagel. In order to secure Igraine, Uther killed the duke, and disguised himself as the duke through magic. In this way, he was able to sleep with Igraine and father a child before they were married. Merlin, the king's sorcerer, had foretold all this and had advised Uther to have the child brought up by a loyal knight, Sir Ector. Merlin brought the baby to Sir Ector and his wife, who christened the boy Arthur and brought him up with no knowledge of his royal lineage.

Some time later, the king fell into a fever. When it was clear that Uther would soon die Merlin gathered all the knights and barons of the realm to the king's deathbed, where the king named Arthur as his heir to the throne. Although all had heard the king's words, none save Merlin knew who Arthur was.

A Christmas Miracle

Unable to find the king's chosen heir, many of the most powerful English barons felt that they should now be king, and it seemed that bloody civil war would be the only outcome. However, Merlin quickly instructed the Archbishop of Canterbury to tell all the lords of the land to assemble in London on Christmas Day, when a miracle would reveal the successor to Uther Pendragon.

After they had prayed with the archbishop, the lords came out of church to find a great marble stone in the churchyard. Set in the stone was a mighty steel anvil, and buried up to its hilt in the anvil was a mighty war sword that bore the legend:

'He who pulls this sword from the stone and anvil is the true and rightful king of all England.'

A New Year's Tournament

None of the assembled lords could loose the sword from its sheath of steel and stone, however, until a new king appeared who could do so, the lords were duty bound to stay in London. To pass the time they announced that a grand tournament would be held on New Year's Day where the finest warriors in the land would complete for fabulous prizes.

News of this great tournament and of the sword in the stone spread quickly, and Sir Ector determined to see the spectacle accompanied by his son the young Sir Kay and Arthur, who had just been made his squire. When they arrived at the tournament, Sir Kay realized that in his haste he had come without his sword and sent Arthur back for it.

Arthur Brings Kay a Sword — But Not His Own

When Arthur got back to his home, he found the whole place locked and shuttered, everyone having left for the tournament. Faithful squire that he was, he knew he could not return to his lord without a sword, and he thought long and hard about where he might get one. At last he knew that the only sword he could bring was the sword buried in the anvil set in the stone. In haste he rode to the church, entered the churchyard and, without further thought, pulled the sword from the anvil.

When Sir Kay saw the sword that his squire had brought him, he knew at once that this was the sword from the stone, the most important sword in the kingdom.

The Sword Is Replaced in the Stone

At first Kay claimed the sword for himself, but when his father asked him to swear the true story of how he came by the sword Kay confessed that it was Arthur, his squire, who had brought it to him. Faithful Sir Ector now realized that the baby that Merlin had given him so many years ago was Uther Pendragon's son and heir to the throne of all England. To be doubly certain, Ector asked Arthur to replace the sword in the stone. Ector could not move the sword one inch, but once again Arthur effortlessly pulled the sword free.

Ector explained to the archbishop that his foster son Arthur had pulled the sword from the stone. Again Arthur replaced the sword in the stone, and this time each of the assembled lords tried to pull it free, and each of the assembled lords failed.

England Crowns a New King

On the feast of Pentecost, for the final time Arthur approached the stone and slid the sword free of the anvil. Now there could be no doubt that this was indeed the true heir to Uther Pendragon's throne. Merlin confirmed as much, revealing that Arthur's true father was the dead king Uther.

Now all knelt before Arthur, who was first made knight and then crowned king by the archbishop. So began the wise and glorious reign of Arthur, King of England.

Picture Credits

All pictures courtesy of the below, and the creative manipulation of Lucy Robins.

Recommended Reading

Ford, Patrick K. (ed./trans.), *The Mabinogi and Other Medieval Welsh Tales*,
University of California Press, 1997.

Gray, Elizabeth A. (ed./trans.), *Cath Maige Tuired: The Second Battle of Mag Tuired*,
Irish Texts Society, 1983.

Green, Miranda, *Dictionary of Celtic Myth and Legend*, Thames and Hudson, 1997

Kinsella, Thomas (trans.), *The Tain*, Oxford University Press, 1970.

Koch, John T. and John Carey, *The Celtic Heroic Age: Literary Sources for Ancient Celtic Europe & Early Ireland & Wales*, Celtic Studies Publications, 2003.

Mac Cana, Proinsias, *Celtic Mythology*, Chancellor Press, 1996.

MacKillop, James, *Myths and Legends of the Celts*, Penguin Books, 2005

O'Sullivan, Sean, *Folktales of Ireland*, University of Chicago Press, 1966.

Rees, Alwyn and Brinley, *Celtic Heritage: Ancient Tradition in Ireland and Wales*,
Thames and udson, 1961.

Ross, Anne, *Druids, Gods & Heroes*, Peter Lowe, 1986

Index

Index